The Cessation of Mind

Commentaries of the Yoga Sutras of Patanjali

CW01560444

OSHO

The Cessation of Mind

DIAMOND POCKET BOOKS

ISBN : 81-7182-094-8

Publishers	: **Diamond Pocket Books (P) Ltd.**
	X-30, Okhla Industrial Area,
	Phase-II, New Delhi-110020
Phone	: 011-51611861
Fax	: 011-51611866
E-mail	: sales@diamondpublication.com
Website	: www.diamondpublication.com

The Cessation of Mind

Copyright © 1996 Osho International Foundation
All rights reserved

Osho® is a registered trademark of Osho International Foundation, used under license.

Originally published in English under the title:
The Path of Yoga, Chapters 1-5
Copyright © 1976 Osho International Foundation
All rights reserved

Editing by Ma Ananda Prem & Ma Yoga Sudha
Coordination by Swami Amano Manish

| Edition | : 2005 |
| Price | : Rs. 50/- |

Design & Lay out: Media Pulse, Delhi-92

| Printed at | : Adarsh Printers, Delhi-110032 |

No part of this book may be reproduced or transmitted in any form or by any means electronic or mechanical including photocopying or recording or by any information storage and retrieval system without permission in writing from **Osho International Foundation.**

Contents

1

INTRODUCTION TO THE PATH OF YOGA

1. अथ योगानुशासनम्।

Now the discipline of yoga.

2. योगश्चित्तवृत्ति निरोधः।

Yoga is the cessation of mind.

3. तदा द्रष्टुः स्वरूपेऽ वस्थानम्।

Then the witness is established in itself.

4. वृत्ति सारूप्यमितंरत्र।

In the other states there is identification with the modifications of the mind.

We live in a deep illusion—the illusion of hope, of future, of tomorrow. As man is, man cannot exist without self-deception.

Nietzsche says somewhere that man cannot live with the true: he needs dreams, he needs illusions, he needs lies to exist. And Nietzsche is true. As man is he cannot exist with the truth. This has to be understood very deeply, because without understanding it there can be no entry into the inquiry which is called Yoga.

The mind has to be understood deeply—the mind which needs lies, the mind which needs illusions, the mind which cannot exist with the real, the mind which needs dreams. You are not only dreaming in the night; even while awake you are continuously dreaming. You may be looking at me, you may be listening to me, but a dream current goes on within you. The mind is continuously creating dreams, images, fantasies.

Now scientists say that a man can live without sleep but he cannot live without dreams. In the old days it was understood that sleep was a necessity, but now modern research says sleep is not really a necessity; sleep is needed only so that you can dream. Dreaming is the necessity. If you are allowed to sleep but not allowed to dream, you will not feel fresh, alive, in the morning. You will feel tired, as if you have not been able to sleep at all.

In the night there are periods—periods for deep sleep and periods for dreaming. There is a rhythm, just like day and night. There is a rhythm: in the beginning you fall into deep sleep for nearabout forty, forty-five minutes, then the dream phase comes in; then you dream; then again dreamless sleep, then again dreaming. This goes on the whole night. If your sleep is disturbed while you are deeply asleep without dreaming, in the morning you will not feel that you have missed anything. But while you are dreaming if your dream is disturbed then in the morning you will feel completely tired, exhausted.

Now this can be known from the outside. If someone is sleeping you can judge whether he is dreaming or asleep. If he is dreaming his eyes will be continuously moving, as if he is seeing something with closed eyes. When he is fast asleep the eyes will not move; they will remain steady. So if your sleep is disturbed while your eyes are moving, in the morning you will feel tired. While your eyes are not moving sleep can be disturbed; in the morning you will not feel anything is missing.

Many researchers have proved that the human mind feeds on dreams; dreaming is a necessity, and dreaming is total auto-deception. And this is so not only in the night: while awake also the same pattern follows. Even in the day you can notice—sometimes there will be dreams floating in the mind, sometimes there will be no dreams.

When there are dreams you will be doing something but you will be absent. Inside you are occupied. For example, you are here. If your mind is passing through a dream-state you will listen to me without listening at all, because your mind will be occupied within. If you are not in a dreaming state, only then can you listen to me.

Day and night, mind goes on moving from no-dream to dream, then from dream to no-dream again. This is an inner rhythm. Not only do we continuously dream, in life also we project hopes into the future.

The present is almost always a hell: you can prolong this hell only because of the hope that you have projected into the future. You can live today because of the tomorrow. You are hoping something is going to happen tomorrow—some doors of paradise will open tomorrow. They never open today, and when tomorrow will come it will not come as tomorrow, it will come as today, but by that time your mind has moved again. You go on moving ahead of you: this is what dreaming means. You are not one with the real, that which is nearby, that which is here and now, you are somewhere else—moving ahead, jumping ahead.

And that tomorrow, that future, you have named it in so many ways. People call it heaven, some people call it moksha, but it is always in the future. Somebody is thinking in terms of wealth, but that wealth is going to be in the future. And somebody is thinking in terms of paradise, and that paradise is going to be after you are dead—far away in the future. You waste your present for that which is not: this is what dreaming means. You cannot be here and now. To be just in the moment seems to be arduous.

You can be in the past, because again that is dreaming—memories, remembrance of things which are no more—or you can be in the future, which is projection, which again is creating something out of the past. The future is nothing but the past projected again—more colorful, more beautiful, more pleasant, but it is the past refined.

You cannot think anything other than the past: the future is nothing but the past projected again—and both are not. The present is, but you are never in the present. This is what dreaming means. And Nietzsche is right when he says that man cannot live with the truth. He needs lies, he lives through lies. Nietzsche says that we go on saying that we want the truth, but no one wants it. Our so-called truths are nothing but lies, beautiful lies. No one is ready to see the naked reality.

This mind cannot enter on the path of Yoga because Yoga means a methodology to reveal the truth. Yoga is a method to come to a non-dreaming mind. Yoga is the science to be in the here and now. Yoga means now you are ready not to move into the future. Yoga means now you are ready not to hope, not to jump ahead of your being. Yoga means to encounter the reality as it is.

So one can enter Yoga, or the path of Yoga, only when he is totally frustrated with his own mind as it is. If you are still hoping that you can gain something through your mind, Yoga is not for you. A total frustration is needed—the revelation that this mind which projects is futile, the mind that hopes is nonsense, it leads nowhere. It simply closes your eyes, it intoxicates you, it never allows reality to be revealed to you. It protects you against reality.

Your mind is a drug. It is against that which is. So unless you are totally frustrated with your mind, with your way of being, with the way you have existed up to now... if you can drop it unconditionally, then you can enter on the path.

So many become interested but very few enter, because your interest may be just because of your mind. You may be hoping that now, through Yoga, you may gain something, but the achieving motive is there——that you may become perfect through Yoga, you may reach to the blissful state of perfect being, you may become one with the Brahman, you may achieve the satchitananda.... This may be the cause of why you are interested in Yoga. If this is the cause then there can be no meeting between you and the path which is Yoga. Then you are totally against it, moving in a totally opposite dimension.

Yoga means: "Now no hope, now no future, now no desires. But I am ready to know what is. I am not interested in what can be, what should be, what ought to be. I am not interested! I am interested only in that which is"——because only the real can free you, only the reality can become liberation.

Total despair is needed. That despair is called dukkha by Buddha. If you are really in misery don't hope, because your hope will only prolong the misery. Your hope is a drug. It can help you to continue, but where are you moving? It will help you to reach only death and nowhere else. All your hopes can lead you only to death——they are leading.

Become totally hopeless——no future, no hope. Difficult... it needs courage to face the real. But such a moment comes to everyone, sometime or other. A moment comes to every human being when he feels total hopelessness. Absolute meaninglessness happens to him. When he becomes aware that whatsoever he is doing is useless, wheresoever he is going he is going to nowhere, all life is meaningless——suddenly hopes drop. Future drops, and for the first time you are in tune with the present, for the first time you are face to face with reality.

Unless this moment comes to you... you can go on doing asanas, postures; that is not Yoga. Yoga is an inward turning. It is a total about-turn. When you are not moving into the future, not moving towards the past, then you start moving within yourself—because your being is here and now, it is not in the future. You are present here and now, you can enter this reality. But then mind has to be here.

This moment is indicated by the first sutra of Patanjali. Before we talk about the first sutra, a few other things have to be understood.

Yoga is not a religion, remember that. Yoga is not Hindu, it is not Mohammedan. Yoga is a pure science just like mathematics, physics or chemistry. Physics is not Christian, physics is not Buddhist. If Christians have discovered the laws of physics, then too physics is not Christian. It is just accidental that Christians have come to discover the laws of physics. But physics remains just a science. Yoga is a science—it is just an accident that Hindus discovered it. It is not Hindu. It is a pure mathematics of the inner being. So a Mohammedan can be a yogi, a Christian can be a yogi, a Jaina, a Buddhist can be a yogi.

Yoga is pure science. And Patanjali is the greatest name as far as the world of Yoga is concerned. This man is rare, there is no other name comparable to Patanjali. For the first time in the history of humanity this man brought religion to the status of a science. He made religion a science; pure laws, no belief is needed.

So-called religions need beliefs. There is no other difference between one religion and another; the difference is only of beliefs. A Mohammedan has certain beliefs, a Hindu certain others; a Christian certain others. The difference is of beliefs. Yoga has nothing as far as belief is concerned; Yoga doesn't say to believe in anything. Yoga says "Experience." Just as science says "Experiment," Yoga says "Experience." Experiment and experience are both the same; their directions are different. Experiment means there is something you can do outside; experience means there is something you can do inside. Experience is an inner experiment.

Science says, 'Don't believe, doubt as much as you can," but also, Don't disbelieve"—because disbelief is again a sort of belief. You can believe in God, you can believe in the concept of no-God. You can say God is with a fanatic attitude; you can say quite the reverse, that God is not, with the same fanaticism. Atheists, theists, are all believers, and belief is not the realm for science. Science means to experience something, that which is; no belief is needed.

So the second thing to remember is that Yoga is existential, experiential, experimental. No belief is required, no faith is needed—only courage to experience—and that's what is lacking. You can believe easily because in belief you are not going to be transformed. Belief is something added to you, something superficial. Your being is not changed, you are not passing through some mutation. You may be a Hindu—you can become a Christian the next day. You simply change, you change the Gita for a Bible. You can change it for a Koran, but the man who was holding the Gita and is now holding the Bible remains the same. He has changed his beliefs.

Beliefs are like clothes. Nothing substantial is transformed, you remain the same. Dissect a Hindu, dissect a Mohammedan—inside they are the same. The Hindu goes to a temple, the Mohammedan hates the temple. The Mohammedan goes to the mosque and the Hindu hates the mosque but inside they are the same human beings.

Belief is easy because you are not really required to do

anything, just a superficial dressing, a decoration, something which you can put aside any moment you like. Yoga is not belief; that's why it is difficult, arduous—and sometimes it seems impossible. It is an existential approach. You will come to the truth not through belief but through your own experience, through your own realization. That means you will have to be totally changed—your viewpoints, your way of life, your mind; your psyche as it is has to be shattered completely. Something new has to be created. Only with that new will you come in contact with the reality.

So Yoga is both a death and a new life. As you are you will have to die, and unless you die the new cannot be born. The new is hidden in you. You are just a seed for it and the seed must fall down, be absorbed by the earth. The seed must die, only then will the new arise out of you. Your death will become your new life. Yoga is both a death and a new birth. Unless you are ready to die you cannot be reborn. So it is not a question of changing beliefs.

Yoga is not a philosophy. I say it is not a religion and I say it is not a philosophy. It is not something you can think about. It is something you will have to be; thinking won't do. Thinking goes on in your head. It is not really deep into the roots of your being, it is not your totality. It is just a part, a functional part. It can be trained and you can argue logically, you can think rationally, but your heart will remain the same. Your heart is your deepest center, your head is just a branch. You can be without the head but you cannot be without the heart. Your head is not basic.

Yoga is concerned with your total being, with your roots. It is not philosophical. So with Patanjali we will not be thinking, speculating. With Patanjali we will be trying to know the ultimate laws of being, the laws for its transformation, the laws of how to die and how to be reborn again, the laws for a new order of being. That is why I call it a science.

Patanjali is rare. He is an enlightened person like Buddha, like Krishna, like Christ, like Mahavira, Mohammed, Zarathustra, but he is different in one way. Buddha, Krishna, Mahavira, Zarathustra, Mohammed—none of them has a scientific attitude. They are great founders of religions. They have changed the whole pattern of the human mind and its structure, but their approach is not scientific.

Patanjali is like an Einstein in the world of buddhas. He is a phenomenon. He could easily have been a Nobel Prize winner like an Einstein or Bohr or Max Planck or Heisenberg. He has the same attitude, the same approach as a rigorous, scientific mind. He is not a poet; Krishna is a poet. He is not a moralist; Mahavira is a moralist. He is basically a scientist who is thinking in terms of laws. And he has come to deduce absolute laws of the human being, the ultimate working structure of the human mind and of reality.

And if you follow Patanjali you will come to know that he is as exact as any mathematical formula. Simply do what he says and the result will happen. The result is bound to happen—it is just like two plus two become four; it is just like you heat water up to one hundred degrees and it evaporates. No belief is needed, you simply do it and know. It is something to be done and known. That's why I say there is no comparison: never again has a man existed on this Earth like Patanjali.

You can find poetry in Buddha's utterances; it is bound to be there. Many times while Buddha is expressing himself he becomes poetic. The realm of ecstasy, the realm of ultimate knowing is so beautiful, the temptation is so strong to become poetic... the beauty is such, the benediction is such, the bliss is such that one starts talking in poetic language.

But Patanjali resists that. It is very difficult, no one else has been able to resist. Jesus, Krishna, Buddha, they all became poetic. When the splendor, the beauty explode within you, you will start dancing, you will start singing. In that state you are just like a lover who has fallen in love with the whole universe.

Patanjali resists that. He will not use poetry; he will not even use a single poetic symbol. He will not do anything with poetry. He will not talk in terms of beauty: he will talk in terms of mathematics, he will be exact. And he will give you maxims— those maxims are just indications of what is to be done. He will not explode into ecstasy, he will not say things that cannot be said, he will not try the impossible. He will just put down the foundation and if you follow the foundation you will reach the peak which is beyond. He is a rigorous mathematician, remember this.

The first sutra:
'Now the discipline of Yoga.

Athayoganushasanam: Now the discipline of Yoga.
Each single word has to be understood, because Patanjali will not use a single superfluous word.

Now the discipline of Yoga... First try to understand the word 'now'. This 'now' is an indication to the state of mind I was just talking to you about.

If you are disillusioned, if you are hopeless, if you have completely become aware of the futility of all desires; if you see your life as meaningless; whatsoever you have been doing up to now has simply fallen dead, nothing remains in the future, you are in absolute despair—what Kierkegaard calls anguish—you are in anguish, suffering, not knowing what to do, not knowing where to go, not knowing to whom to turn, just on the verge of madness or suicide or death, your whole pattern of life has suddenly become futile; if this moment has come, Patanjali says, "Now the discipline of Yoga"—only now can you understand the science of Yoga, the discipline of Yoga.

If that moment has not come you can go on studying Yoga: you can become a great scholar but you will not be a yogi. You can write theses on it, you can give discourses on it, but you will not be a yogi. The moment has not come for you. Intellectually you can become interested, through your mind you can be related to Yoga, but Yoga is nothing if it is not a discipline. Yoga is not a shastra; it is not a scripture. It is a discipline, it is something you have to do. It is not curiosity, it is not philosophical speculation. It is deeper than that—it is a question of life and death.

If the moment has come when you feel that all directions have become confused, all roads have disappeared, the future is dark and every desire has become bitter and through every desire you have known only disappointment, all movement into hopes and dreams has ceased: Now the discipline of Yoga.

This 'now' may not have come. Then I may go on talking about Yoga but you will not listen. You can listen only if the moment is present in you. Are you really dissatisfied? Everybody will say yes, but that dissatisfaction is not real. You are dissatisfied with this, you may be dissatisfied with that, but you are not totally dissatisfied. You are still hoping. You are dissatisfied because of your past hopes but you are still hoping for the future. Your dissatisfaction is not total: you are still hankering for some satisfaction somewhere, for some gratification somewhere.

Sometimes you feel hopeless but that hopelessness is not true. You feel hopeless because certain hopes have not been achieved, certain hopes have fallen away—but hoping is still there, hoping has not fallen away. You will still hope. You are dissatisfied with this hope, that hope, but you are not dissatisfied with hope as such. If you are disappointed with hope as such the moment has come, and then you can enter Yoga. And then this entry will not be an entering into a mental, speculative phenomenon. This entry will be an entry into a discipline.

What is discipline? Discipline means what creates an order within you. As you are you are a chaos. As you are you are totally disorderly. Gurdjieff used to say—and Gurdjieff is in many ways like Patanjali, he was again trying to make the core of religion a science—Gurdjieff said that you are not one, you are a crowd; not even when you say "I", is there any I. There are many I's in you, many egos. In the morning one I, in the afternoon another I, in the evening a third I, but you never become aware of this mess—because who will become aware of it? There is not a center that can become aware.

The discipline of Yoga means Yoga wants to create a crystallized center in you. As you are you are a crowd and a crowd has many phenomena. One is that you cannot believe a crowd. Gurdjieff used to say that man cannot promise: who will promise? You are not there. If you promise who will fulfill the promise? Next morning the one who promised is no more.

People come to me and they say, "Now I will take the vow. I promise to do this," and I tell them, "Think twice before you promise something. Are you confident that the next moment the one who promised it will be there?" You decide from tomorrow to get up early in the morning at four o'clock, and at four o'clock somebody in you says, "Don't bother. It is so cold outside. And why are you in such a hurry? We can do it tomorrow"—and you fall asleep again. When you get up you repent and you think, "This is not good. I should have done it." You decide again, "Tomorrow I will do it"; and the same is going to happen tomorrow because at four in the morning the one who promised is no more there, somebody else is in the chair. You are a Rotary Club: the chairman goes on changing and every member becomes a Rotary chairman. There is rotation: every moment someone else is the master.

Gurdjieff used to say, "This is the chief characteristic of man—that he cannot promise." You cannot fulfill a promise. You go on giving promises, and you know well that you cannot fulfill them because you are not one; you are a disorder, a chaos. Hence Patanjali says, "Now the discipline of Yoga." If your life has become an absolute misery, if you have realized that whatsoever you do creates hell, then the moment has come. This moment can change your dimension, your direction of being.

Up until now you have lived as a chaos, a crowd. Yoga means now you will have to be a harmony, you will have to become one. A crystallization is needed, a centering is needed. And unless you attain a center all that you do is useless; it is wasting life and time. A center is the first necessity, and only a person who has a center can be blissful. Everybody asks for it. But you cannot ask—you have to earn it! Everybody hankers for a blissful state of being. But only a center can be blissful, a crowd cannot be blissful. A crowd has got no self, there is no atman.

Who is going to be blissful?

Bliss means absolute silence, and silence is possible only when there is harmony—when all the discordant fragments have become one, when there is no crowd, but one. When you are alone in the house and nobody else is there, you will be blissful. Right now everybody else is in your house, you are not there. Only the guests are there, the host is always absent—and only the host can be blissful.

This centering Patanjali calls discipline, anushasanam. The word 'discipline' is beautiful. It comes from the same root as the word 'disciple'. 'Discipline' means the capacity to learn, the capacity to know. But you cannot know, you cannot learn unless you have attained the capacity to be.

One man once went to Buddha and he said… he must have been a social reformer, a revolutionary… he said to Buddha, "The world is in misery. I agree with you."

Buddha has never said that the world is in misery. Buddha says you are the misery, not the world; life is misery, not the world; man is misery, not the world; mind is misery, not the world. But that revolutionary said, "The world is in misery, I agree with you. Now tell me, what can I do? I have a deep compassion and I want to serve humanity."

Service must have been his motto! Buddha looked at him and remained silent. Buddha's disciple, Ananda, said, "This man seems to be sincere. Guide him. Why are you silent?"

Then Buddha said to that revolutionary, "You want to serve the world, but where are you? I don't see anyone inside. I look in you—there is no one. You don't have any center, and unless you are centered whatsoever you do will create more mischief."

All your social reformers, your revolutionaries, your leaders, they are the great mischief creators, mischief-mongers. The world would be better if there were no leaders. But they can-not help: they must do something because the world is in misery and they are not centered, so whatsoever they do will create more misery. Compassion alone will not help, service alone will not help. Compassion through a centered being is something totally different. Compassion through a crowd is mischief; that compassion is poison.

Now the discipline of Yoga.

'Discipline' means the capacity to be, the capacity to know, the capacity to learn. We must understand these three things.

The capacity to be…. All the Yoga postures are not really concerned with the body, they are concerned with the capacity to be. Patanjali says if you can sit silently without moving your body for a few hours, you are growing in the capacity to be. Why do you move? You cannot sit without moving even for a few seconds: your body starts moving, somewhere you feel itching, the legs go dead, many things start happening—these are just excuses for you to move.

You are not a master. You cannot say to the body, "Now I will not move for one hour." The body will revolt immediately! Immediately it will force you to move, to do something. And it will give reasons: "You have to move because an insect is biting." You may not find the insect when you look. You are not a being, you are a trembling—a continuous hectic activity. Patanjali's asanas, postures, are not really concerned with any kind of physiological training but with an inner training of being: just to be, without doing anything, without any movement, without any

23

activity. Just remain—that remaining will help centering.

If you can remain in one posture the body will become a slave; it will follow you. And the more the body follows you the more you will have a greater being within you, a stronger being within you. And remember, if the body is not moving your mind cannot move, because mind and body are not two things. They are two poles of one phenomenon. You are not body and mind, you are bodymind. Your personality is psychosomatic, bodymind, both. The mind is the most subtle part of the body. Or you can say the reverse, that body is the most gross part of the mind. So whatsoever happens in the body happens in the mind and vice versa, whatsoever happens in the mind happens in the body. If the body is non-moving and you can attain a posture, if you can say to the body, "Keep quiet," the mind will remain silent. Really, the mind starts moving and tries to move the body, because if the body moves then the mind can move. In a non-moving body the mind cannot move; it needs a moving body.

If the body is non-moving, the mind is non-moving—you are centered. This non-moving posture is not only a physiological training, it is just to create a situation in which centering can happen, in which you can become disciplined. When you are, when you have become centered, when you know what it means to be, then you can learn because then you will be humble. Then you can surrender. Then no false ego will cling to you because once centered you know all egos are false. Then you can bow down. Then a disciple is born.

To become a disciple is a great achievement. Only through discipline will you become a disciple. Only through being centered will you become humble, will you become receptive, will you become empty and the guru, the master, can pour himself

24

into you. In your emptiness, in your silence, he can come and reach to you. Communication becomes possible.

A disciple means one who is centered, humble, receptive, open, ready, alert, waiting, prayerful. In Yoga the master is very, very important, absolutely important, because only when you are in the close proximity of a being who is centered will your own centering happen.

That is the meaning of satsang. You have heard the word satsang'; it is totally wrongly used. Satsang means, in close proximity to the truth; it means, near the truth, it means near a master who has become one with the truth—just being near him, open, receptive and waiting. If your waiting has become deep, intense, a deep communion will happen.

The master is not going to do anything. He is simply there, available. If you are open he will flow within you. This flowing is called satsang. With a master you need not learn anything else. If you can learn satsang, that's enough—if you can just be near him without asking, without thinking, without arguing; just present there, available, so the being of the master can flow in you.... And being can flow. It is already flowing. Whenever a person achieves integrity his being becomes a radiation. He is flowing. Whether you are there to receive or not, that is not the point. He flows like a river. If you are empty like a vessel, ready, open, he will flow in you.

A disciple means one who is ready to receive, who has become a womb... the master can penetrate into him. This is the meaning of the word satsang. It is not basically a discourse; satsang is not a discourse. There may be a discourse but the discourse is just an excuse. You are here and I will talk on Patanjali's sutras—that is just an excuse. If you are really here then the discourse, the talk, becomes just an excuse for your being here, for you to be here. And if you are really here, satsang starts. I can flow, and that flow is deeper than any talk, any communication through language, than any intellectual meeting with you.

While your mind is engaged… if you are a disciple, if you are a disciplined being, if your mind is engaged in listening to me, then your being can be in satsang. Then your head is occupied. If your heart is open then on a deeper level a meeting happens. That meeting is satsang, and everything else is just an excuse just to find ways to be close to the master.

Closeness is all—but only a disciple can be close. Anybody and everybody cannot be close. Closeness means a loving trust. Why are we not close?—because there is fear. Too close may be dangerous, too open may be dangerous, because you become vulnerable and then it will be difficult for you to defend. So just as a security measure we keep everybody, we never allow anyone to enter a certain distance.

Everybody has a territory around him. Whenever somebody enters your territory you become afraid. Everybody has a space to protect. You are sitting alone in your room, a stranger enters into the room: just watch when you become really scared. There is a point… if he enters that point, beyond that point you will become scared, you will be afraid. A sudden trembling will be felt. He can move beyond a certain territory.

To be close means that now you have no territory of your own. To be close means to be vulnerable; to be close means that whatsoever happens, you are not thinking in terms of security.

A disciple can be close for two reasons. One: he is a

centered one, he is trying to be centered. A person who is even trying to be centered becomes unafraid; he becomes fearless. He has something which cannot be killed. You don't have anything, hence the fear. You are a crowd. The crowd can disperse at any moment. You don't have something like a rock which will be there whatsoever happens. You are existing without a rock, without a foundation—a house of cards, bound to be always in fear. Any wind, even any breeze can destroy you, so you have to protect yourself.

Because of this constant protection you cannot love, you cannot trust, you cannot be friendly. You may have many friends but there is no friendship, because friendship needs closeness. You may have wives and husbands and so-called lovers but there is no love, because love needs closeness, love needs trust. You may have gurus, masters but there is no disciplehood, because you cannot allow yourself to be totally given to somebody's being; nearness to his being, closeness to his being, so he can overpower you, flood over you.

A disciple means a seeker who is not a crowd, who is trying to be centered and crystallized—at least trying, making efforts, sincere efforts to become individual, to feel his being, to become his own master. The whole discipline of Yoga is an effort to make you a master of yourself. As you are, you are just a slave of many, many desires. Many, many masters are there and you are just a slave—and pulled in many directions.

Now the discipline of Yoga.

Yoga is discipline. It is an effort on your part to change yourself. Many other things have to be understood. Yoga is not a therapy. In the West many psychological therapies are now prevalent, and many Western psychologists   think that Yoga is also a therapy. It is not! It is a discipline. And what is   the difference? This is the difference: a therapy is needed if you are ill, a therapy is needed if you are diseased, a therapy is needed if you are pathological. A discipline is needed even when you are healthy. Really, only when you are healthy can a discipline then help. It is not for pathological cases.

Yoga is for those who are completely healthy as far as medical science is concerned, normal. They are not schizophrenic, they are not mad, they are not neurotic. They are normal people, healthy people with no particular pathology. Still they become aware that whatsoever is called normality is futile, whatsoever is called health is of no use. Something more is needed, something greater is needed, something holier and whole is needed.

Therapies are for ill people. Therapies can help you to come to Yoga, but Yoga is not a therapy. Yoga is for a higher order of health, a different order of health——a different type of being and wholeness. Therapy can, at the most, make you adjusted. Freud says we cannot do more. We can make you an adjusted, normal member of the society——but if the society itself is pathological, then? And it is! The society itself is ill. A therapy can make you normal in the sense that you are adjusted to the society, but society itself is ill.

So sometimes it happens that in an ill society a healthy person is thought to be ill. A Jesus is thought to be ill and every effort is done to make him adjusted. And when it is found that he is a hopeless case then he is crucified. When it is found that nothing can be done, that this man is incurable, then he is crucified. The society is itself ill because society is nothing but your collective. If all the members are ill the society is ill, and every member has to be adjusted to it.

Yoga is not therapy, Yoga is not trying in any way to make you adjusted to the society. If you want to define Yoga in terms of adjustment then it is not adjustment with the society, but it is adjustment with existence itself. It is adjustment with the divine.

So it may happen that a perfect yogi may appear mad to you. He may look out of his senses, out of his mind, because now he is in touch with the greater, with a higher mind, a higher order of things. He is in touch with the universal mind. It has always happened so: a Buddha, a Jesus, a Krishna, they always look somehow eccentric. They don't belong to us, they seem to be outsiders.

That's why they call them avataras, outsiders. They have come as if from some other planet, they don't belong to us. They may be higher, they may be good, they may be divine, but they don't belong to us. They come from somewhere else. They are not part and parcel of our being, mankind. The feeling has persisted that they are outsiders. They are not—they are the real insiders because they have touched the innermost core of existence. But to us they appear so.

Now the discipline of Yoga.

If your mind has come to realize that whatsoever you have been doing up to now was just senseless, it was a nightmare at the worst or a beautiful dream at the best, then the path of discipline opens before you. What is that path? The basic definition is:

Yoga is the cessation of mind—chittavrittinirodha.

I told you that Patanjali is just mathematical. In a single sentence, "Now the discipline of Yoga," he is finished with you. This is the only sentence that has been used for you. Now he takes it for granted that you are interested in Yoga not as a hope but as a discipline, as a transformation right here and now. He proceeds to define:

Yoga is the cessation of mind.

This is the definition of Yoga, the best. Yoga has been defined in many ways; there are many definitions. Some say Yoga is the meeting of the mind with the divine; hence, it is called Yoga—Yoga means meeting, joining together. Some say that Yoga means dropping the ego, ego is the barrier: the moment you drop the ego you are joined to the divine. You were already joined; only because of the ego it appeared that you were not joined. And there are many definitions, but Patanjali's is the most scientific. He says, "Yoga is the cessation of mind."

Yoga is the state of no-mind. The word 'mind' covers all—your egos, your desires, your hopes, your philosophies, your religions, your scriptures. 'Mind' covers all. Whatsoever you can think is mind. All that is known, all that can be known, all that is knowable, is within mind. Cessation of the mind means cessation of the known, cessation of the knowable. It is a jump into the unknown. When there is no-mind you are in the unknown. Yoga is a jump into the unknown. It will not be right to say 'unknown'; rather, 'unknowable'.

What is the mind? What is the mind doing there? What is it?

Ordinarily we think that mind is something substantial there, inside the head. Patanjali doesn't agree—and no one who has ever known the insides of the mind will agree. Modern science also doesn't agree. Mind is not something substantial inside the head. Mind is just a function, just an activity.

You walk, and I say you are walking. What is walking? If you stop, where is walking? If you sit down, where has the walking gone? Walking is nothing substantial; it is an activity. So while you are sitting no one can ask, "Where have you put your walking? Just now you were walking, so where has the walking gone?" You will laugh. You will say, "Walking is not something substantial, it is just an activity. I can walk. I can again walk and I can stop. It is activity."

Mind is also activity, but because of the word 'mind' it appears as if something substantial is there. It is better to call it 'minding'—just like walking. Mind means 'minding', mind means thinking. It is an activity.

Again and again I have been quoting Bodhidharma....

He went to China and the emperor of China went to see him. And the emperor said, "My mind is very uneasy, very disturbed. You are a great sage and I have been waiting for you. Tell me what I should do to put my mind at peace."

Bodhidharma said, "Don't do anything. First, you bring your mind to me."

The emperor could not follow. He said, "What do you mean?"

He said, "Come in the morning at four o'clock, when nobody is here. Come alone—and remember to bring your mind with you."

The emperor couldn't sleep the whole night. Many times he

canceled the whole idea: "This man seems to be mad. What does he mean, 'Come with your mind, don't forget'?" But the man was so enchanting, so charismatic that he couldn't cancel the appointment. As if a magnet were pulling him, at four o'clock he jumped out of the bed and said, "Whatsoever happens, I must go. This man may have something, his eyes say that he has something. Looks a little crazy... but still I must go and see what can happen."

So he arrived, and Bodhidharma was sitting with his big staff. And he said, "So you have come? Where is your mind? Have you brought it or not?"

The emperor said, "You talk nonsense. When I am here my mind is here, and it is not something which I can forget somewhere. It is in me."

So Bodhidharma said, "Okay. So the first thing is decided— that the mind is within you."

The emperor said, "Okay, the mind is within me."

Bodhidharma said, "Now close your eyes and find out where it is. And if you can find out where it is, immediately indicate to me. I will put it at peace."

So the emperor closed his eyes, tried and tried, looked and looked. The more he looked the more he became aware that there is no mind, that mind is an activity. It is not something there so you can pinpoint it. But the moment he realized that it is not something, then the absurdity of his quest became exposed to him: "If it is not something, nothing can be done about it. If it is an activity, then don't do the activity; that's all. If it is like walking, don't walk."

He opened his eyes. He bowed down to Bodhidharma and said, "There is no mind to be found."

Bodhidharma said, "Then I have put it at peace. And whenever you feel that you are uneasy, just look within for where that uneasiness is."

The very looking is anti-mind, because a look is not a thinking. And if you look intensely your whole energy becomes a look, and the same energy becomes movement and thinking.

Yoga is the cessation of mind.

This is Patanjali's definition: when there is no mind you are in Yoga, when there is mind you are not in Yoga. So you may do all the postures but if the mind goes on functioning, if you go on thinking, you are not in Yoga.

Yoga is the state of no-mind. If you can be without the mind without doing any posture, you have become a perfect yogi. It has happened to many without doing any postures, and it has not happened to many who have been doing postures for many lives. Because the basic thing to be understood is: when the activity of thinking is not there...you are there when the activity of the mind is not there. When thoughts have disappeared—they are just like clouds—when they have disappeared your being, just like the sky, is uncovered. It is always there—only covered with the clouds, only covered with thoughts.

Yoga is the cessation of mind.

Now in the West there is much appeal for Zen—a Japanese method of Yoga. The word 'Zen' comes from dhyana. Bodhidharma introduced this word 'dhyana' into China. The word 'dhyana' became jhan, and then in China ch'an, and then

33

the word traveled to Japan and became 'Zen'.

The root is 'dhyana'. 'Dhyana' means no-mind, so the whole training of Zen in Japan is nothing but how to stop 'minding', how to be a no-mind, how to be simply without thinking. Try it! When I say try it, it will look contradictory, because there is no other way to say it. Because if you try, the very trying, the effort, is coming from the mind. You can sit in a posture and you can try some japa, chanting, a mantra, or you can just try to sit silently, not to think. But then 'not to think' becomes the thinking. Then you go on saying, "I am not to think, don't think, stop thinking," but this is all thinking.

Try to understand. When Patanjali says no-mind,... cessation of mind, he means complete cessation. He will not allow you to make a mantra, "Ram-Ram-Ram." He will say that this is not cessation, you are using the mind. He will say, "Simply stop!" But you will ask, "How? How can you simply stop?" The mind continues. Even if you sit the mind continues. Even if you don't do it goes on doing.

Patanjali says, "Then just look. Let mind go, let mind do whatsoever it is doing. You just look. You don't interfere. You just be a witness. You just be an onlooker, not concerned, as if the mind doesn't belong to you, as if it is not your business, not your concern. Don't be concerned! Just look and let the mind flow. It is flowing because of past momentum, because you have always helped it to flow. The activity has taken its own momentum, so it is flowing. Just don't cooperate. Look, and let the mind flow."

For many, many lives, maybe a million lives, you have cooperated with it, you have helped it, you have given your energy to it. The river will flow awhile. If you don't cooperate, if you just look, unconcerned—Buddha's word is 'indifference', upeksha: looking without any concern, just looking, not doing anything in any way—the mind will flow for a while and it will stop by itself. When the momentum is lost, when the energy has flowed, the mind will stop. When the mind stops you are in Yoga: you have attained the discipline. This is the definition:

Yoga is the cessation of mind.
Then the witness is established in itself.

When the mind ceases, the witness is established in itself.

When you can simply look without being identified with the mind, without judging, without appreciating, condemning, without choosing; you simply look and the mind flows, a time comes when by itself, of itself, the mind stops.

When there is no-mind you are established in your witnessing. Then you have become a witness, just a seer, a drashta, a sakshi. Then you are not a doer, then you are not a thinker. Then you are simply being, pure being, purest of being. Then the witness is established in itself.

In the other states there is identification with the modifications of the mind.

Except witnessing, in all states you are identified with the mind. You become one with the flow of thoughts, you become one with the clouds: sometimes with the white cloud, sometimes with the black cloud, sometimes with a rain-filled cloud, sometimes with a vacant, empty cloud. But whatsoever, you become one with the thought, you become one with the cloud, and you miss the purity of your sky, the purity of space. You become clouded and this clouding happens because you get identified, you become one.

A thought comes. You are hungry and the thought flashes in the mind. The thought is simply that there is hunger, the stomach is feeling hunger. Immediately you get identified; you say, "I am hungry." The mind was just filled with a thought that hunger is there, you have become identified and you say, "I am hungry." This is identification.

Buddha also feels hunger, Patanjali also feels hunger, but Patanjali will never say that, "I am hungry": he will say, "The body is hungry"; he will say, "My stomach is feeling hungry"; he will say, "There is hunger. I am a witness. I have come to witness this thought which has been flashed by the belly into the brain that 'I am hungry.'" The belly is hungry, Patanjali will remain a witness. You become identified, you become one with the thought.

Then the witness is established in itself. In the other states there is identification with the modifications of the mind.

This is the definition:
Yoga is the cessation of mind.

When mind ceases you are established in your witnessing self. In other states except this there are identifications. And all identifications constitute the sansar; they are the world. If you are in the identifications you are in the world, in the misery. If you have transcended the identifications you are liberated. You have become a siddha, you are in nirvana. You have transcended this world of misery and entered the world of bliss.

And that world is here and now—right now, this very moment! You need not wait for even a single moment. Just become a witness of the mind and you have entered. Get identified with the mind and you have missed. This is the basic definition.

Remember everything, because later on, in other sutras, we will go into details about what is to be done, how it is to be done.

But always keep in mind that this is the foundation: one has to achieve a state of no-mind, that is the goal.

Enough for today?

2

DESIRELESS, YOU ARE ENLIGHTENED

The first question:
You said last night that total despair,
frustration and hopelessness is the
beginning ground for yoga. This
gives yoga a pessimistic look.
Is this pessimistic state really
necessary to begin the path
of yoga? Does an optimist
also begin with the
path of yoga?

It is neither: it is not pessimistic, it is not optimistic, because pessimism and optimism are two aspects of the same coin. A pessimist means one who was an optimist in the past; an optimist means one who will be a pessimist in the future. All optimism leads to pessimism because every hope leads to hopelessness.

If you are still hoping then Yoga is not for you. The desire is there, hope is there; sansar, the world is there. Your desire is the world, your hope is the bondage, because hope will not allow you to be in the present. It will go on forcing you towards the future; it will not allow you to be centered. It will pull and push but it will not allow you to remain in a restful moment, in a state of stillness. It will not allow you.

So when I say total hopelessness I mean that hope has failed and hopelessness also has become futile. Then it is total hopelessness. Total hopelessness means even hopelessness is not there, because when you feel hopeless a subtle hope is there. Otherwise why should you feel hopeless? Hope is there, you are still clinging to it, hence the hopelessness.

Total hopelessness means now there is no hope. And when there is no hope there cannot be hopelessness. You have simply

41

dropped the whole phenomenon. Both aspects have been thrown, the whole coin has been dropped. In this state of mind you can enter the path of Yoga, never before. Then there is no possibility: hope is against Yoga.

Yoga is not pessimistic. You may be optimistic or pessimistic; Yoga is neither. If you are pessimistic you cannot enter on the path of Yoga because a pessimist clings to his miseries. He will not allow his miseries to disappear. An optimist clings to his hopes and a pessimist clings to his miseries, to his hopelessness. That hopelessness has become the companion. Yoga is for the one who is neither, who has become so totally hopeless that even to feel hopelessness is futile.

The opposite can be felt only if you go on clinging with the positive somewhere deep down. If you cling to hope you can feel hopelessness. If you cling to expectation you can feel frustration. If you simply come to realize that there is no possibility to expect anything, then where is the frustration? Then this is the nature of existence, that there is no possibility to expect anything, there is no possibility for hope. When this becomes a certainty, how can you feel hopeless? Then both have disappeared.

Patanjali says, "Now the discipline of Yoga": that 'now' will happen only when you are neither. Pessimistic attitudes or optimistic attitudes, both are ill. But there are teachers who go on talking in terms of optimism, particularly American Christian missionaries. They go on talking in terms of hope, optimism, future, heaven. In the eyes of Patanjali that is just juvenile, childish, because you are simply giving a new disease. You are substituting a new disease for the old. You are unhappy and somehow you are seeking happiness. So whosoever gives you an assurance that, "This is the path that will lead you to happiness," you will follow it. He is giving you hope—but you are feeling so much misery because of your past hopes. He is again creating a future hell.

Yoga expects you to be more adult, more mature. Yoga says there is no possibility to expect anything; there is no possibility of any fulfillment in the future. There is no heaven in the future waiting for you and no God waiting for you with Christmas gifts. There is nobody waiting for you so don't hanker after the future.

And when you become aware that there is nothing which is going to happen somewhere in the future...you will become alert here and now because there is nowhere to move. Then there is no way to tremble. Then a stillness happens to you. Suddenly you are in a deep rest. You cannot go anywhere; you are at home. Movement ceases, restlessness disappears. Now is the time to enter Yoga.

Patanjali will not give you any hope. He respects you more than you respect yourself. He thinks you are mature and toys will not help. It is better to be alert to what is the case. But immediately when I say, "Total hopelessness" your mind will say, "This appears pessimistic," because your mind lives through hope, your mind clings to desires, expectations.

You are so miserable right now that you will commit suicide if there is no hope. Really, if Patanjali is true, what will happen to you? If there is no hope, no future and you are thrown back to your present, you will commit suicide. Then there is nothing to live for. You live for something which will happen somewhere, sometime. It is not going to happen, but the feeling that it may happen helps you to be alive.

That's why I say when you have come to a point where suicide has become a meaningful thing, where life has lost all its meaning, where you can kill yourself, in that moment Yoga becomes possible because you will not be ready to transform yourself unless this intense futility of life has happened to you. You will be ready to transform yourself only when you feel there is no way—either suicide or sadhana, either commit suicide or transform your being. When only two alternatives are left, only then is Yoga chosen, never before. But Yoga is not pessimistic. You are optimistic, then Yoga appears to you as pessimistic. It is because of you.

In the West Buddha has been taken as the peak of pessimism because Buddha says life is dukkha, anguish. So Western philosophers have been commenting on Buddha that he is a pessimist. Even a person like Albert Schweitzer, a person we can expect to know certain things, even he is in confusion. He thinks the whole East is pessimistic and this is a great criticism for him. The whole East—Buddha, Patanjali, Mahavira, Lao Tzu, they are all pessimists for him. They appear so! They appear so because they say your life is meaningless. Not that they say life is meaningless, but the life that you know. And unless this life becomes absolutely meaningless you cannot transcend it, you will cling to it.

And unless you transcend this life, this mode of existence, you will not know what bliss is. But Buddha or Patanjali, they will not talk much about bliss just because they have a deep compassion for you. If they start talking about bliss you again create a hope. You are incurable: you again create a hope. You say, "Okay! Then we can leave this life. If a more abundant life, a richer life is possible, then we can leave desires. If through leaving desires the deepest desire of reaching to the ultimate, the peak of bliss, is possible, then we can leave desires. But we can leave only for a greater desire."

Then where are you leaving? You are not leaving at all. You are simply substituting a different desire for the old one. And the new desire will be more dangerous than the old because you are

44

already frustrated with the old. To get frustrated with the new you may again take even a few lives to come to a point where you can say God is useless, where you can say heaven is foolish, where you can say all future is nonsense.

It is not a question of worldly desires, it is a question of desire as such. Desiring must cease. Only then you become ready, only then you gather courage, only then the door opens and you can enter into the unknown. Hence, Patanjali's first sutra: Now the discipline of Yoga.

The second question:
It is said that Yoga is an atheistic system. Do you agree with this?

Again, Yoga is neither. It is a simple science. It is neither theistic nor atheistic. Patanjali really is superb, a miracle of a man. He never talks about God. And even if he mentions God once, then too he says it is just one of the methods of reaching the ultimate. The belief in God is just a method to reach the ultimate—there is no God. To believe in God is just a technique, because through believing in God prayer becomes possible; through believing in God surrender becomes possible. The significance is of surrender and prayer, not of God.

Patanjali is really unbelievable! He said God—the belief in God, the concept of God—is also one of the methods among many methods to reach the truth. Ishwara pranidhan—to believe in God is just a path. But it is not a necessity. You can choose something else. Buddha reaches to that ultimate reality without believing in God. He chooses a different path where God is not needed.

You have come to my house, you have passed through a certain street—that street was not the goal, it was just instrumental. You could have reached to the same house through some other street; others have reached through other streets. On your street there may be green trees, big trees, on other streets there are not. So God is just one path. Remember the distinction: God is not the goal. God is just one of the paths.

Patanjali never denies, he never assumes. He is absolutely scientific. It is difficult for Christians to think how Buddha could attain the ultimate truth, because he never believed in God. It is difficult for Hindus to believe how Mahavira could attain liberation; he never believed in God.

Before the Western thinkers became alert about Eastern religions they always defined religion as God-centered. When they came upon Eastern thinking and they became aware that there has been a traditional path, a godless path reaching toward truth, they were shocked: "It is impossible!"

H. G. Wells has written about Buddha that Buddha is the most godless man and yet the most godly. He never believed and he will never tell anybody to believe in any God, but he himself is the suprememost phenomenon of the happening of divine being. Mahavira too travels a path where God is not needed.

Patanjali is absolutely scientific: he says we are not related with means, there are a thousand and one means—the goal is the truth. Some have achieved it through God, so it is okay—believe in God and achieve the goal, because when the goal is achieved you will throw your belief. So belief is just instrumental. If you don't believe it is okay, don't believe, and travel the path of beliefflessness and reach the goal.

He is neither theist nor atheist. He is not creating a religion, he is simply showing you all the paths that are possible and all the laws that work in your transformation. God is one of those paths, it is not a must. If you are godless there is no need to be non-religious. Patanjali says you can also reach—be godless, don't bother about God. These are the laws and these are the experiments; this is the meditation—pass through it.

He does not insist on any concept. It was very difficult. That's why the Yoga Sutras of Patanjali are rare, unique. Such a book has never happened before and there is no possibility again, because whatsoever can be written about Yoga he has written, he has left nothing out. No one can add anything to it. Never in the future is there any possibility to create another work like Patanjali's Yoga Sutras. He has finished the job completely, and he could do this so totally because he is not partial. If he were partial then he could not do it so totally.

Buddha is partial, Mahavira is partial, Jesus is partial, Mohammed is partial—they have a certain path. And their partiality may be because of you, because of a deep compassion for you. They insist on a certain path, they go on insisting their whole life. And they say, "Everything else is wrong, this is the right path," just to create faith in you. You are so faithless, you are so filled with doubt that if they say, "This path leads, others' paths also lead," you will not follow any. They insist that only this path leads.

This is not true. This is just a device for you because if you feel any uncertainty in them, if they say, "This also leads, that also leads; this is also true, that is also true," you will become uncertain. You are already uncertain. You need someone who is absolutely certain. Just to look certain to you they have pretended to be partial.

But if you are partial you cannot cover the whole ground. Patanjali is not partial. He is less concerned with you, more concerned with the past designs of the path. He will not use a lie; he will not use a device, he will not compromise with you. No scientist can compromise.

Buddha can compromise. He has compassion, he is not treating you scientifically. A very deep human feeling is there for you. He can even lie just to help you—and you cannot understand the truth—he compromises with you.

Patanjali will not compromise with you. Whatsoever is the fact, he will talk about the fact. And he will not descend a single step to meet you, he is absolutely uncompromising. Science has to be. Science cannot compromise, otherwise it will itself become a religion. He is neither atheist nor theist. He is neither Hindu nor Mohammedan nor Christian nor Jaina nor Buddhist. He is absolutely a scientific seeker just revealing whatsoever is the case, revealing without any myth. He will not use a single parable. Jesus will go on talking in stories because you are children and you can only understand stories. He will talk in parables. Buddha uses so many stories just to help you to attain a little glimpse.

I was reading about a Hassid, a Jewish master, Baal Shem. He was a rabbi in a small village, and whenever there was some trouble, some disease, some calamity in the village, he would move into the forest. He would go to a certain spot under a certain tree and there he would do some ritual and then he would pray to God. And it always happened that the calamity would leave the village, the illness would disappear from the village, the trouble would go.

Then Baal Shem died. So his successor.... The problem came again—the village was in trouble. There was some calamity and the villagers asked the successor, the new rabbi, to go to the forest and pray to God. The new rabbi was very much disturbed because he didn't know the spot, the exact tree. He was unacquainted, but still he went under any tree. He burned the fire, did the ritual and prayed and said to God, "Look, I don't know the exact spot my master used to come to, but you know. You are omnipotent, you are omnipresent, so you know—so there is no need to seek for the exact spot. My village is in some trouble, so listen and do something." The calamity was gone.

Then when this rabbi died and his successor was there again the problem came. The village was in a certain crisis and they came. The rabbi was disturbed, he had even forgotten the prayer. So he went into the forest, chose any place. He didn't know how to burn the ritual fire but anyhow he burned the fire and said to God, "Listen, I don't know how to burn the ritual fire, I don't know the exact spot and I have forgotten the prayer. But you are all-knowing so you know already; there is no need for me to know. So do whatsoever is needed." And he came back and the village passed through the crisis.

Then he also died. His successor.... And the village was again in trouble, so they came. He was sitting in his armchair. He said, "I don't want to go anywhere. Listen, you are everywhere. I don't know the prayer, I don't know any ritual. But that doesn't matter; my knowing is not the point. You know everything. What is the use of praying and what is the use of a ritual and what is the use of a particular sacred spot? I know only the story of my successors. I will tell you the story, that this happened in Baal Shem's time, then his successor, then his successor: this is the story. Now do the right thing and this is enough." And the calamity disappeared. It is said that God loved the story so much.

People love their stories, and the people's God also, and through stories you can have certain glimpses. But Patanjali will not use a single parable. I told you he is just Einstein plus Buddha, a very rare combination. He has the inner witnessing of Buddha and the mechanism of the mind of an Einstein——he is neither.

Theism is a story, atheism is the anti-story. They are just myths, man-created parables. To some the one appeals, to some the other. Patanjali is not interested in stories, not interested in myths. He is interested in the naked truth. He will not even clothe it, he will not put on any dressing, he will not decorate it. That is not his way, remember this.

We will move on a very dry land, a desert-like land. But the desert has its own beauty. It has no trees, it has no rivers, but it has a vastness of its own. No forest can be compared to it. Forests have their own beauties, hills have their own beauties, rivers their own beauties. Desert has its own vast infinity.

We will be moving through desert-land. Courage is needed. He will not give you a single tree to rest under. He will not give you any story, just the bare facts. He will not use even a single superfluous word. Hence the word 'sutras'. 'Sutras' means the basic minimum.

A sutra is not even a complete sentence. It is just the essential——just as when you make a telegram you go on cutting out superfluous words. Then it becomes a sutra because only ten words or nine words can be put in it. If you were going to write a letter you would fill ten pages, and even in ten pages the message would not be complete. But in a telegram in ten words it is not only complete, it is more than complete. It hits the heart, the very essence is there.

These are telegrams——Patanjali's sutras. He is a miser, he will not use a single superfluous word. So how can he tell stories?—he cannot. And don't expect it. So don't ask whether he is a theist or an atheist; those are stories.

Philosophers have created many stories, and it is a game. If you like the game of atheism, be an atheist. If you like the game of theism, be a theist. But these are games, not the reality. Reality is something else. Reality is concerned with you, not what you believe. The reality is you, not what you believe. The reality is behind the mind, not in the contents of the mind. Because theism is a content of the mind, atheism is a content of the mind, something in the mind. Hinduism is a content of the mind or Christianity is a content of the mind.

Patanjali is concerned with the beyond, not with the content. He says, "Throw this whole mind. Whatsoever it contains, it is useless." You may be carrying beautiful philosophies; Patanjali will say, "Throw them! All is rubbish." It is difficult. If someone says, "Your Bible is rubbish, your Gita is rubbish, your scriptures are rubbish, rot, throw them," you will be shocked. But this is how it is going to happen. Patanjali cannot make any compromise with you. He is uncompromising and that's the beauty. And that is his uniqueness.

The third question:

You talked about the significance of discipleship on the path of Yoga, but how can an atheist be a disciple?

Neither a theist nor an atheist—they cannot be disciples. They have already taken an attitude, they have already decided, so what is the point of being a disciple? If you already know how can you be a disciple? Discipleship means the realization that, "I don't know." Atheists, theists—no, they cannot be disciples.

And if you believe in something you will miss the beauty of disc, iplehood. If you know something already that knowing will give you ego; it will not make you humble. That's why pundits and scholars miss. Sometimes sinners have reached, but scholars never. They know too much, they are so clever. Their cleverness is their disease, that becomes the suicide. They won't listen because they will not be ready to learn.

Disciplehood simply means an attitude to learn, a moment-to-moment remaining aware that "I don't know." This knowing that "I don't know," this awareness that "I am ignorant" gives you opening. Then you are not closed. The moment you say "I know" you are a closed circle, the door is no longer open. But when you say "I don't know" it means you are ready to learn. It means the door is open.

If you have already reached, concluded, you cannot be a disciple. One has to be in a receptive mood. One has to be completely aware that the real is unknown, "And whatsoever I know is trivial, is just rubbish." What do you know? You may have gathered much information but that is not knowledge. You may have accumulated much dust through universities; that is not knowledge. You may know about Buddha, you may know about Jesus, but that is not knowledge. Unless you become a Buddha there is no knowledge. Unless you are a Jesus there is no knowledge.

Knowledge comes through being, not through memory. You can have a trained memory; memory is just a mechanism. It will not give you a richer being. It may give you nightmarish dreams but it will not give you a richer being. You will remain the same, covered with much dust. Knowledge, and particularly the ego that comes through knowledge—the feeling that "I know"—closes you. Now you cannot be a disciple. And if you cannot be a disciple you cannot enter the discipline of Yoga. So come to the door of Yoga ignorant—alert of your ignorance, alert that you don't know. And I will tell you: this is the only knowledge which will help, the knowledge that "I don't know."

This will make you humble. A subtle humility will come to you. The ego, by and by, will subside. Knowing that you don't know, how can you be egoistic? Knowledge is the most subtle food for the ego: you feel you are something. You know, you become somebody.

Just two days ago I initiated a girl from the West into sannyas and I gave her a name, Yoga Sambodhi, and I asked her, "Will it be easy for you to pronounce?" She said, "Yes. It looks just like the English word 'somebody'. But sambodhi is quite the opposite. When you become nobody, then sambodhi happens. Sambodhi means enlightenment. If you are somebody, sambodhi will never happen. That 'somebodiness' is the barrier.

When you feel you are nobody, when you feel you are nothing, suddenly you are available for many mysteries to happen to you. Your doors are open. The sun can rise, the sunrays can penetrate you. Your gloom, your darkness, will disappear. But you are closed. The sun may be knocking on the door but there is no opening, not even a window is open.

Atheists or theists, Hindus or Mohammedans, Christians or Buddhists, they cannot enter on the path. They believe! They have already reached Buddha without reaching anywhere. They have concluded without any realization. They have words in the mind, concepts, theories, scriptures—and the more the burden, the more dead they are.

The fourth question:

You said that Yoga does not ask for any faith. But if a disciple needs faith, surrender and trust in the master as a basic condition, then how is the first statement valid?

No, I never said that Yoga doesn't ask for faith. I said Yoga doesn't ask for any belief. Faith is totally different, trust is totally different. Belief is an intellectual thing. But faith is a very deep intimacy, it is not intellectual. You love a master, then you trust and there is faith. But this faith is not in any concept, it is in the very person. And this is not a condition, it is not required. Remember this distinction: it is not required that you must have faith in the master, it is not a precondition. All that is said is this: if trust happens between you and the master, then satsang will be possible. It is just a situation, not a condition. Nothing is required.

Just as love… if love happens then marriage can follow—but you cannot make love a condition that first you must love and then marriage will follow. But then you will ask, "How can one love?" If it happens it happens, if it is not happening it is not happening. You cannot do anything. So you cannot force trust.

In the old days seekers would roam all over the world. They would roam from one master to another, just waiting for the phenomenon to happen. You cannot force it. You may pass through many masters just in search if somewhere something clicks. Then the thing has happened; it is not a condition. You cannot go to a master and try to trust him. How can you try to trust? The very trying, the very effort, shows you don't trust. How can you try to love someone? Or can you? If you try, the whole thing has become false. It is a happening.

But unless this happens satsang will not be possible. Then the master cannot give his grace to you. Not that he will prevent himself from giving—you are not available. He cannot do anything, you are not open.

The sun may be waiting near the window but if it is closed, what can the sun do? The rays will reflect back. They will come, knock on the door, and go back. Remember, it is not a condition that you open the door and the sun will rise—it is not a condition! The sun may not be there, it may be night. Just by opening your door you cannot create the sun. Your opening of the door is just your being available: if the sun is there he can enter.

So seekers will move, will have to move from one master to another. The only thing to remember is, they must remain open and they should not judge. If you come near a master and you don't feel any tuning with him, move—but don't judge, because your judgment will be wrong. You have never been in contact. Unless you love you don't know, so don't judge. Simply say, "This master is not for me, I am not for this master. The thing has not happened." You simply move.

If you start judging then you are closing yourself for other masters also. You may have to pass through many, many situations, but remember this: don't judge. Whenever you feel that something is wrong with the master, move on. That means you cannot trust. Something has gone wrong, you cannot trust. But don't say the master is wrong—you don't know! You simply move on, that's enough. You seek somewhere else.

If you start judging, condemning, concluding, then you will be closed. And these eyes which judge will never be able to trust. Once you have become a victim of judgment you will never be able to trust because you will find something or other which will help you not to trust, which will give you a closing.

So don't trust, don't judge, move on. Someday, if you go on moving, the thing is bound to happen. Someday, somewhere, in some moment—because there are moments; you cannot do anything about them. When you are vulnerable and when the master is flowing… you are vulnerable, you meet. In a certain point of time and space, the meeting happens. Then satsang becomes possible.

Satsang means to be in close proximity with a master, with a man who has known, because then he can flow. He is already flowing. Sufis say that that's enough; just to be in close proximity to a master, that is enough. Just to sit near him, just to walk by the side of him, just to sit outside his room, just to watch in the night sitting outside his wall, just to go on remembering… that's enough.

But it takes years, these years of waiting…. And he will not treat you well, remember—he will create every type of hindrance. He will give you many chances to judge. He will spread rumors about himself so you can think that he is wrong and you can escape. He will help you in every way to escape. Unless you pass all these hurdles… and they are necessary, because a cheap trust is of no use. A trust, a seasoned trust which has waited long has become a strong rock… only then can the deepest layers be penetrated.

Patanjali doesn't say that you will have to believe. Belief is intellectual. You believe in Hinduism, it is not your trust. It is just that accidentally you were born in a Hindu family. And so you have heard; from the very childhood you have been impregnated. You have been impressed with theories, concepts, philosophies, systems. They have become part of your blood. They have just fallen into your unconscious, you believe in them. But that belief is of no use because it has not transformed you. It is a dead thing, borrowed.

Trust is never a dead thing. You cannot borrow trust from your family; it is a personal phenomenon. You will have to come to it. Hinduism is traditional, Mohammedanism is traditional.

That's why the sangham, the first group around Mohammed, they were the real Mohammedans because it was a trust for them; they had come personally to the master. They had lived with the master in close proximity, they had satsang. They believed in Mohammed, and Mohammed is not a man to be easily trusted—difficult. If you had been to Mohammed you would have had to… he had nine wives, impossible to believe in such a man. He had a sword in his hand and on his sword was written, "Peace is the motto"; the word 'islam' means peace. How can you believe this man?

You can believe in a Mahavira when he says, "Non-violence"; he is non-violent. Obviously, you can believe in Mahavira. How can you believe in Mohammed with a sword? And he says, "Love is the message and peace is the motto." You cannot believe. This man is creating hurdles.

He was a Sufi; he was a master. He would create every difficulty. So if your mind still functioned—you doubted, you were skeptical—you could escape. But if you remained, waited, if you had patience—and infinite patience will have been needed—someday you would come to know Mohammed, you would become a Mohammedan. Just by knowing him you would become a Mohammedan.

The first group of disciples was a totally different thing. The first group of disciples of Buddha was a totally different thing. Now Buddhists are dead, Mohammedans are dead. They are traditionally Mohammedans.

Truth cannot be transferred like property. Your parents cannot give you truth. They can give you property because the property belongs to the world. Truth doesn't belong to the world, they cannot give it to you; they cannot have it as a treasure. They cannot have it in the bank so that it can be transferred to you. You will have to seek on your own. You will have to suffer and you will have to become a disciple and you will have to pass through rigorous discipline. It will be a personal happening. Truth is always personal: it happens to a person. Trust is different, belief is different. Belief is given by others, trust is earned by yourself.

Patanjali doesn't require any belief. But without trust nothing can be done, without trust nothing is possible. But you cannot force it. Understand, you cannot force your trust, it is not in your hands to force it. If you force it will be false. And no trust is better than a false trust, because you are wasting yourself. It is better to move somewhere else where the real can happen.

Don't judge, go on moving: someday, somewhere, your master is waiting. And the master cannot be shown to you—"Go here and this will be your master." You will have to seek, you will have to suffer, because through suffering and seeking you will be able to see him. Your eyes will become clear. The tears will disappear, your eyes will be unclouded and you will realize that this is the master.

It is reported: one of the Sufis named Junnaid went to an old fakir and he asked him, "I have heard that you know. Show me the path."

The old man said, "You have heard that I know. You don't know. Look at me and feel."

The man said, "I cannot feel anything. Just do one thing, just show me the path where I can find my master."

So the old man said, "You go first to Mecca. Do the

pilgrimage and search for such and such a man. He will be sitting under a tree. His eyes will be such, they will be throwing light, and you will feel a certain perfume like musk around him. Go and seek."

And Junnaid traveled and traveled for twenty years. Wherever he heard there was a master, he would go. But neither was the tree there, nor the perfume, the musk, nor those eyes the old man has described. The personality was not there. And he had a readymade formula, so he would judge immediately, "This is not my master," and he would move on. After twenty years he reached under a tree—the master was there. The musk was floating in the air just like a haze around the man. The eyes were fiery, a red light was flowing. This was the man! He fell at his feet and said, "Master, I have been searching for you for twenty years."

The master said, "I have also been waiting for you for twenty years. Look again."

He looked—this was the same man who twenty years before had told him the way to find the master. Junnaid started weeping. He said, "What? You played a joke on me? Twenty years wasted! Why couldn't you say that you are my master?"

The old man said, "That would not have helped. That would not have been of much use because unless you have eyes to see.... These twenty years helped you to see me, I am the same man. But twenty years before you told me that 'I don't feel anything.' I am the same, but now you have become capable to feel. You have changed. These twenty years rubbed you hard—all the dust has fallen, your mind is clear. This fragrance of musk was also there that time but you were not capable of smelling it. Your nose was closed, your eyes were not functioning, your heart was not really beating so contact was not possible."

You don't know, and nobody can say where the trust will happen. I don't say, trust the master. I simply say find the person where trust happens—that person is your master. And you cannot do anything about it. You will have to wander. The thing is certain to happen, but the seeking is necessary because seeking prepares you. Not that the seeking leads you to the master: seeking prepares you so that you can see. He may be just near you....

The fifth question:

Last night you spoke of satsang and the importance of the disciple's proximity to the guru. Does this mean physical proximity? Is the disciple who lives at a great physical distance from the guru at a loss?

Yes and no! Yes, a physical closeness is necessary in the beginning because as you are you cannot understand anything else right now. You can understand the body, you can understand the language of the physical. You exist at the physical, so yes, a physical closeness is necessary—in the beginning.

And I say no also because as you grow, as you start learning a different language which is of the non-physical, then physical closeness is not necessary. Then you can go anywhere. Then space doesn't make any difference, you remain in contact. Not only space, but time also doesn't make any difference. A master may be dead, you remain in contact. He may have dropped his physical body, you remain in contact. If a trust happens, then both time and space are transcended.

Trust is the miracle. You can be in closeness with Mohammed or Jesus or Buddha right now if trust is there. But it is difficult! It is difficult because you don't know how. You cannot trust a living person, how can you trust a dead one? But if trust happens, then you are close to Buddha right now. And for persons who have faith, Buddha is alive. No master ever dies for those who can trust. He goes on helping, he is always there. But for you, even if Buddha is there physically standing behind you or in front of you, just sitting by your side, you are not close to him. There may be vast space between you. Love, trust, faith, they destroy both space and time.

In the beginning, because you cannot understand any other language, you can understand only the language of the physical, physical closeness is necessary—but only in the beginning. A moment will come when the master himself will send you away. He will force you to go away because that too becomes necessary—you may start clinging to the physical language.

Gurdjieff almost always, all his life, would send his disciples away. He would create such a miserable situation for them, then they would have to leave. It would be impossible to live with him. After a certain point he would help them to go away. He would really force them to go away, because you should not become too much dependent on the physical. The other, the higher language, must develop. You must start feeling close to him wherever you are, because the body has to be transcended. Not yours only—the master's body has also to be transcended.

But in the beginning it is a great help. Once the seeds are sown, once they have taken root, then you are strong enough. Then you can go away and then you can feel. If just by going away the contact is lost, then the contact is not very important. Trust will grow more the further you go away. Trust will grow more, because wherever you are on the earth you will start feeling the master's presence continuously. The trust will grow. He will be helping you now through hidden hands, invisible hands. He will be working on you through your dreams and you will feel that constantly, like a shadow, he is following you.

But that is a very developed language. Don't try it from the very beginning because then you can deceive. So I will say, move step by step. Wherever trust happens, then close your eyes and follow blindly. Really, the moment trust happens you have closed your eyes. Then what is the use of thinking, arguing? Trust has happened and trust will not listen to anything now. Then follow, and remain close unless the master himself sends you away. And when he sends you away then don't cling. Then follow, follow his instruction and go away, because he knows better. And he knows what is helpful.

Sometimes just being near the master it may become difficult for you to grow, just as under a big tree a new seed will have many difficulties to grow. Under a big tree a new tree will become crippled. Even trees take care to throw their seed far away so that the seeds can sprout. The trees use many tricks to send the seed away. Otherwise they will die if they fall down just under the big tree; there is so much shadow, no sun reaches there, no sunrays reach.

So a master knows better. If he feels that you should go away, then don't resist. Then simply follow and go away. This going away will be a coming nearer to him. If you can follow, if you can silently follow without any resistance, then this going away will be a coming nearer. You will attain a new closeness.

The sixth question:

When you ask us to understand something clearly, whom do you address to understand? Mind has to cease. Therefore, it is no use making the mind understand anything. Who should understand then?

Yes, mind has to cease, but it has not ceased yet. Mind has to be worked on. An understanding has to be created in the mind: through that understanding this mind will die. That understanding is just like poison: you take the poison—you are the taker and the poison kills you. The mind understands, but the understanding is poison for the mind. That's why the mind resists so much. It tries and tries not to understand. It creates doubt, it fights. In every way it protects itself because understanding is poison for the mind. It is elixir for you, but for the mind it is poison.

So when I say understand clearly, I mean your mind, not you, because you need not have any understanding, you are already understanding. You are the very wisdom, the pragnya. You need no help from me or from anybody else.

Your mind has to be changed. And if understanding happens to the mind, mind will die, and with the mind the understanding will disappear. Then you will be in your purity. Then your being will reveal a mirror-like purity—no content, contentless. But that inner being needs no understanding; it is already the very core of understanding. It needs no understanding—just the clouds of the mind have to be persuaded....

So what is understanding, really?—just a persuasion for the mind to leave. Remember, I don't say fight, I say persuasion. If you fight, the mind will never leave because through fight you show your fear. If you fight you show that the mind is something you are afraid of. Just persuade. All these teachings, all meditations are a deep persuasion for the mind to come to a point where it can commit suicide, where it simply drops, where mind itself becomes such an absurdity that you cannot carry it anymore—you simply drop it. It is better to say mind drops itself.

So when I say clear understanding, I am addressing your mind. And there is no other way. Only your mind can be approached because you are unavailable. You are so hidden deep inside, and just the mind is at the door. The mind has to be persuaded to leave the door and to leave the door open—then you will become available.

I am addressing mind—your mind, not you: If mind drops there is no need to address. I can sit in silence and you will understand; there is no need to address. The mind needs words, the mind needs thoughts, the mind needs something mental which can persuade it. When Buddha or Patanjali or Krishna talk to you, they are addressing your mind.

A moment comes when mind simply becomes aware of the whole absurdity. It is just like this: I see that you are pulling the strings of your shoelaces, trying to pull yourself up by them, and I tell you, "What nonsense you are doing! This is impossible. You cannot pull yourself up just by your own shoelaces. It is simply impossible, it cannot happen." So I persuade you to think more about the whole thing: "This is absurd. What are you doing?" And then you feel miserable because it is not happening. So I go on telling you, insisting, hammering, and one day you may become aware that, "Yes, this is absurd. What am I doing?"

The whole effort of the mind is just like pulling yourself up by your shoelaces. Whatsoever you are doing is absurd. It can never lead you anywhere other than to hell, than to misery. It has always led you to misery—you are still not aware. All this communication from me is just to make your mind alert that the whole effort is absurd. Once you come to feel that the whole effort is absurd, the effort disappears. It is not that you will have to leave your shoelaces and you will have to make some effort and it is going to be arduous: you will simply see the fact and you will leave and you will laugh. If you leave your shoelaces and simply stand and laugh, you have become enlightened. This is going to be the case.

Through understanding the mind drops. Suddenly you become aware that no one else was responsible for your misery, you were creating it; continuously, moment to moment, you were the creator. And you were creating the misery and then you were asking how to go beyond it, how to not be miserable, how to achieve bliss, how to achieve samadhi. And while you are asking you are creating. Even this asking, "How to achieve samadhi?" is creating misery because then you say, "I have been making so much effort and samadhi has not been attained yet. I am doing everything that can be done and the samadhi has not been attained yet. When will I become enlightened?"

Now you are creating a new misery when you have made enlightenment also an object of desire—which is absurd. No desire will come to a fulfillment. When you realize this, desires drop—you are enlightened. Desireless, you are enlightened. With desires you go moving in a circle of misery.

The last question:

You said that Yoga is a science, a methodology for inner awakening. But effo⸱ to be, to go nearer to no-mind, implies motivation and hop⸱ Even to undergo the process of inner transformation implies ⸱otivation. Then how can one move on the path of Yoga without hope and motivation? Does not waiting even imply motivation?

Yes, you cannot move on the path of Yoga with motivation, with desire, with hope. Really, there is no movement on the path of Yoga. When you come to understand that all desire is absurd, all desire is misery... there is nothing to do, because every doing will be a new desire. There is nothing to do! You simply cannot do anything because whatsoever you do will lead you into a new misery. Then you don't do. Desires have dropped, mind has ceased, and this is Yoga. You have entered. This is not a movement, this is a stillness. Because of language problems arise: I say that you have entered, it appears that you have moved. When desire ceases, all movement ceases. You are in Yoga: "Now the discipline of Yoga."

With motivation, in the name of Yoga you will again create other miseries. Every day I see people. They come: "I have been practicing Yoga for thirty years, nothing has happened." But who told you that something is going to happen? He must be waiting for something to happen—that's why nothing has happened. Yoga says, don't wait for the future.

You meditate, but you meditate with the motive that through meditation you will reach somewhere, some goal. You are missing the point. Meditate and enjoy! There is no goal, there is no future, no further; there is nothing ahead. Meditate, enjoy it without any motivation—and suddenly the goal is there. Suddenly the clouds disappear because they were created by your desire. Your motivation is the smoke which creates the clouds... they have disappeared. So play with the meditation; enjoy it. Don't make it a means. It is the end. This is the whole point to be understood.

Don't create new desires. Understand the very nature of desire—that it is misery. Just try to understand the nature of desire and you will come to know that it is misery. Then what is to be done? Nothing is to be done! Becoming alert that desire is misery, desire drops: "Now the discipline of Yoga." You have entered the path.

And it depends on your intensity. If your realization that desire is misery is so deep, so total, you have not only entered Yoga, you have become a siddha. You have reached the goal. It will depend on your intensity. If the intensity is total then you have reached the goal. If your intensity is not so total you have entered the path.

Enough for today?

3

THE FIVE MODIFICATIONS OF MIND

5. वृत्तयः पञ्चतय्यः क्लिष्टाक्लिष्टाः।

*The modifications of the mind
are five.
They can be either a source of misery
or of non-misery.*

6. प्रमाणविपर्ययविकल्पनिद्रास्मृतयः।

*They are right knowledge, wrong
knowledge, imagination, sleep and
memory.*

Mind can be either the source of bondage or the source of freedom. Mind becomes the gate for this world, the entry; it can also become the exit. Mind leads you to hell, mind can also lead you to heaven. So it all depends how the mind is used. Right use of mind becomes meditation, wrong use of the mind becomes madness.

Mind is there, with everyone. The possibility of darkness and light, both are implied in it. Mind itself is neither the enemy nor the friend. You can make it a friend, you can make it an enemy; it depends on you—on you who is hidden behind the mind. If you can make the mind your instrument, your slave, the mind becomes the passage through which you can reach the ultimate. If you become the slave and the mind is allowed to be the master, then this mind which has become master will lead you to ultimate anguish and darkness.

All the techniques, all the methods, all the paths of Yoga, are really deeply concerned only with one problem: how to use the mind. Rightly used, mind comes to a point where it becomes no-mind. Wrongly used, mind comes to a point where it is just a chaos, many voices antagonistic to each other, contradictory, confusing, insane.

The madman in the madhouse and Buddha under his bodhi tree—both have used the mind, both have passed through the mind. Buddha has come to a point where mind disappears. Rightly used, it goes on disappearing; a moment comes when it is not. The madman has also used the mind. Wrongly used, mind becomes divided; wrongly used, mind becomes many; wrongly used, it becomes a multitude. And finally the mad mind is there, you are absolutely absent.

Buddha's mind has disappeared and Buddha is present in his totality. A madman's mind has become total and he himself has disappeared completely. These are different... the two poles. You and your mind: if they exist together then you will be in misery. Either you will have to disappear or the mind will have to disappear. If the mind disappears then you achieve truth; if you disappear you achieve insanity. And this is the struggle: who is going to disappear?

Are you going to disappear, or the mind? This is the conflict, the root of all struggle.

These sutras of Patanjali will lead you step by step towards this understanding of the mind: what it is; what types of modes it takes, what types of modifications come into it, how you can use it and go beyond it. And remember, you have nothing else right now, only the mind—you have to use it. Wrongly used you will go on falling into more and more misery.

You are in misery. That is because for many lives you have used your mind wrongly and the mind has become the master; you are just a slave, a shadow following the mind. You cannot say to the mind, "Stop!" You cannot order your own mind; your mind goes on ordering you and you have to follow it. Your being has become the shadow and the slave, an instrument.

Mind is nothing but an instrument, just like your hands or your feet. You order your feet—your legs, they move. When you say stop, they stop. You are the master. If I want to move my hand, I move it. If I don't want to move, I don't move it. The hand cannot say to me, "Now I want to be moved." The hand cannot say to me, "Now I will move. Whatsoever you do, I am not going to listen to you." And if my hand starts moving in spite of me, then it will be a chaos in the body. The same has happened in the mind.

You don't want to think and the mind goes on thinking. You want to sleep—you are lying down on your bed, changing sides; you want to go to sleep and the mind continues. The mind says, "No, I am going to think about something"; you go on saying, "Stop!" and it never listens to you. And you cannot do anything. Mind is also an instrument but you have given it too much power. It has become dictatorial, and it will struggle hard if you try to put it in its right place.

Buddha also uses the mind, but his mind is just like your legs. People go on coming to me and they ask, "What happens to the mind of an enlightened one? Does it simply disappear? He cannot use it?"

It disappears as a master, it remains as a slave. It remains as a passive instrument. If a Buddha wants to use it, he can use it. When Buddha speaks to you he will have to use it, because there is no possibility of speech without the mind. The mind has to be used. If you go to Buddha and he recognizes you—that you have also been before—he has to use the mind: without mind there can be no recognition, without mind there is no memory. But he uses the mind, remember—this is the distinction—and you are being used by the mind. Whenever he wants to use it, he uses it.

Whenever he doesn't want to use it, he doesn't use it. It is a passive instrument, it has no hold upon him.

So Buddha remains like a mirror. If you come before the mirror, the mirror reflects you. When you move the reflection is gone, the mirror is vacant. You are not like a mirror. You see somebody: the man has gone but the thinking continues, the reflection continues. You go on thinking about him. And even if you want to stop, the mind won't listen.

Mastery of the mind is Yoga. And when Patanjali says, "Cessation of the mind," this is meant: cessation as a master. Mind ceases as a master. Then it is not active, then it is a passive instrument. You order, it works; you don't order, it remains still. It is just waiting. It cannot assert by itself. The assertion is lost, the violence is lost. It will not try to control you: now just the reverse is the case.

How to become masters? And how to put mind in its right place where you can use it, where if you don't want to use it you can put it aside and remain silent? So the whole mechanism of the mind will have to be understood. Now we should enter the sutra.

The first sutra:
The modifications of the mind are five. They can be either a source of misery or of non-misery.

The first thing to be understood: that mind is not something different from the body, remember. Mind is part of the body. It is body, but deeply subtle; a state of body, but very delicate, very refined. You cannot catch it, but through the body you can influence it. If you take a drug, if you take LSD or marijuana or something else... or alcohol, suddenly the mind is affected. The alcohol goes into the body, not into the mind, but the mind is affected. Mind is the subtlest part of the body.

The reverse is also true: influence the mind and the body is affected. That happens in hypnosis. A person who cannot walk, who says that he has a paralysis, can walk under hypnosis. You don't have paralysis, but if under hypnosis it is said, "Now your body is paralyzed, you cannot walk," you cannot walk. A paralyzed man can walk under hypnosis. What is happening? Hypnosis goes into the mind, the suggestion goes into the mind then the body follows.

First thing to be understood: mind and body are not two. This is one of the deepest discoveries of Patanjali. Now modern science recognizes it, it is very recent in the West. Now they say body-and-mind—to talk in this dichotomy is not right. Now they say it is 'psychosoma', it is mind-body. These two terms are just two functions of one phenomenon. One pole is mind, the other pole is body, so you can work from either and change the other.

The body has five organs of activity, five indriyas, five instruments of activity. The mind has five modifications, five modes of function. Mind and body are one. Body is divided into five functions, mind is also divided into five functions. We will go into each function in detail.

The second thing about this sutra is:
They can be either a source of misery or of non-misery.

These five modifications of the mind, this totality of the mind, can lead you into deep anguish, in dukkha, in misery. Or if you rightly use this mind, its functioning, it can lead you into non-misery.

That word 'non-misery' is very significant. Patanjali doesn't say that it will lead you into ananda, into bliss, no; at the most it can lead you into non-misery. The mind can lead you into misery if you wrongly use it, if you become a slave to it. If you become the master the mind can lead you into non-misery—not into bliss, because bliss is your nature; the mind cannot lead you to it. But if you are in non-misery then the inner bliss starts flowing.

The bliss is always there inside, it is your intrinsic nature. It is nothing to be achieved and earned, it is nothing to be reached somewhere. You are born with it, you have it already, it is already the case. That's why Patanjali doesn't say that the mind can lead you into misery and can lead you into bliss, no. He is very scientific, very accurate. He will not use even a single word which can give you any untrue information. He simply says either misery or non-misery.

Buddha also says many times, whenever seekers will come to him... and seekers are after bliss, so they will ask Buddha, "How can we attain to the bliss, the ultimate bliss?" He will say, "I don't know. I can show you the path which leads to non-misery, just the absence of misery. I don't say anything about the positive, bliss, just the negative. I can show you how to move into the world of non-misery."

That's all that methods can do. Once you are in the state of non-misery the inner bliss starts flowing. But that doesn't come from the mind, that comes from your inner being. So mind has nothing to do with it, mind cannot create it. If mind is in misery then mind becomes a hindrance; if mind is in non-misery then mind becomes an opening—but it is not creative, it is not doing anything.

You open the windows and the rays of the sun enter: by

opening the windows you are not creating the sun, the sun was already there. If it were not there then just by opening the windows, rays wouldn't enter. Your window can become a hindrance: the sunrays may be outside and the window is closed. The window can hinder or it can give way. It can become a passage but it cannot be creative. It cannot create the rays, the rays are there.

Your mind, if it is in misery, becomes closed. Remember, one of the characteristics of misery is closedness. Whenever you are in misery you become closed. Observe—when ever you feel some anguish you are closed to the world. Even to your dearest friend you are closed. Even to your wife, your children, your beloved, you are closed when you are in misery, because misery gives you a shrinking inside. You shrink. From everywhere you have closed your doors.

That's why in misery people start thinking of suicide. Suicide means total closure, no possibility of any communication, no possibility of any door. Even a closed door is dangerous. Someone can open it so destroy the door, destroy all possibilities. Suicide means, "Now I am going to destroy all possibility of any opening. Now I am closing myself totally."

Whenever you are in misery you start thinking of suicide. Whenever you are happy you cannot think of suicide, you cannot imagine, you cannot even think. "Why do people commit suicide? Why? Life is such joy, life is such a deep music, why do people destroy life?"—it appears impossible.

Why, when you are happy, does it look impossible? Because you are open, life is flowing in you. When you are happy you have a bigger soul, expansion. When you are unhappy you have a smaller soul, it shrinks.

When someone is unhappy touch him, take his hand into your hand—you will feel the hand is dead. Nothing is flowing through it—no love, no warmth. It is just cold, as if it belonged to a corpse. When someone is happy touch his hand: there is communication, energy is flowing. His hand is not just a dead end, his hand has become a bridge. Through his hand something comes to you, communicates, relates. A warmth flows. He reaches to you. He makes every effort to flow in you and he allows you also to flow within him.

When two persons are happy they become one. That's why oneness happens in love and lovers start feeling that they are not two. They are two, but they start feeling they are not two because in love they are so happy that a melting happens. They melt into each other, they flow into each other. Boundaries dissolve, definitions are blurred and they don't know who is who. In that moment they become one.

When you are happy you can flow into others and you can allow others to flow in you: this is what celebration means. When you allow everybody to flow in and you flow into everybody, you are celebrating life. And celebration is the greatest prayer, the highest peak of meditation.

In misery you start thinking of committing suicide; in misery you start thinking of destruction. In misery you are at just the opposite pole of celebration—you blame, you cannot celebrate. You have a grudge against everything. Everything is wrong and you are negative and you cannot flow. You cannot relate and you cannot allow anybody to flow into you. You have become an island, closed completely. This is a living death. Life is only when you are open and flowing, when you are unafraid, fearless, open, vulnerable, celebrating.

Patanjali says mind can do two things. It can create misery. You can use it in such a way that you can become miserable... you have used it this way, you are past masters of it. There is no need to talk much about it, you know it already. You know the art of how to create misery. You may not be aware, but that is what you are doing continuously. Whatsoever you touch becomes a source of misery—I say, whatsoever!

I see poor men, they are miserable, obviously. They are poor, the basic needs of life are not fulfilled. But then I see rich men, they are also miserable. And these rich men think that wealth leads nowhere. That is not right. Wealth can lead to celebration—but you don't have the mind to celebrate. So if you are poor you are miserable, if you become rich you are more miserable. The moment you touch the riches you have destroyed them.

You have heard the Greek story of the king Midas? Whatsoever he would touch it would turn into gold. You touch gold, immediately it becomes mud. It is turned into dust and then you think that there is nothing in this world, even riches are useless. They are not. But your mind cannot celebrate, your mind cannot participate in any non-misery. If you are invited into heaven you will not find a heaven there, you will create a hell. As you are, wherever you go you will take your hell with you.

There is one Arabic proverb: that hell and heaven are not geographical places, they are attitudes. And no one enters heaven or hell—everybody enters with heaven or hell. Wherever you go you have your hell projection or the heaven projection with you. You have a projector inside: immediately you project.

But Patanjali is careful: he says misery or non-misery— positive misery or negative misery—but not bliss. Mind cannot give you bliss; no one can give it. It is hidden in you. When mind is in a non-miserable state that bliss starts flowing. It is not coming from the mind, it is coming from beyond. That's why he says they can be either a source of anguish or of non-anguish.

The second sutra:
The modifications of the mind are five....
They are right-knowledge, wrong-knowledge, imagination, sleep and memory.

The first is praman, right-knowledge. The Sanskrit word 'praman' is very deep and really cannot be translated. Right-knowledge is just a shadow, not the exact meaning, because there is no word which can translate praman. Praman comes from the root prama. Many things have to be understood about it.

Patanjali says that the mind has a capacity: if that capacity is directed rightly then whatsoever is known is true, it is self-evidently true. We are not aware about it because we have never used it. That faculty has remained unused. It is just... the room is dark, you come in it, you have a torch, but you are not using it so the room remains dark. You go on stumbling on this table, on that chair, and you have a torch but the torch has to be put on. Once you put the torch on, immediately darkness disappears. And wherever the torch is focused you know: at least that spot becomes evident, self-evidently clear.

Mind has a capacity of praman, of right-knowledge, of wisdom. Once you know it, how to put it on? Then wherever you move that light only right-knowledge is revealed. Without knowing it, whatsoever you know will be wrong.

Mind has the capacity of wrong-knowledge also. In Sanskrit that wrong-knowledge is called viparyaya, false, mithya. And you have that capacity also. You take alcohol, what happens?— the whole world becomes a viparyaya, the whole world becomes false. You start seeing things which are not there. What has happened? Alcohol cannot create things. Alcohol is doing something within your body and brain. The alcohol starts working the center Patanjali calls viparyaya. The mind has a center which can pervert anything. Once that center starts functioning everything is perverted.

I am reminded.... Once it happened that Mulla Nasruddin and his friend were drinking in a pub. They came out, completely drunk. And Nasruddin was an old, experienced drinker; the other was new, so the other was affected more. So the other asked, "Now I cannot see, I cannot hear, I cannot even walk rightly. How will I reach my home? You tell me, Nasruddin. Please direct me. How should I reach my home?"

Nasruddin said, "First you go. After so many steps you will come to a point where there are two ways: one goes to the right, the other goes to the left. You go to the left, because that which goes to the right doesn't exist. I have been many times on that right path also, but now I am an experienced man. You will see two paths—choose the left one, don't choose the right. That right one doesn't exist. Many times I have gone on it and then you never reach, you never reach your home."

Once Nasruddin was teaching his son the first lessons of drinking. So he told him.... The son was asking, he was curious; he asked, "When is one to stop?"

Nasruddin said, "Look at that table. Four persons are sitting there. When you start seeing eight, stop!"

The boy said, "But father, there are only two persons sitting there!"

Mind has a faculty. That faculty functions when you are under the influence of any drug any intoxicant. Patanjali calls that faculty viparyaya, wrong-knowledge, the center of perversion.

Exactly opposite to it there is a center which you don't know. Exactly opposite to it there is a center: if you meditate deeply, silently, that other center will start functioning. That center is called praman, right-knowledge. Through the functioning of that center, whatsoever is known is right. So it is not a question of what you know; from where you know is the question.

That's why all the religions have been against alcohol. It is not on any moralistic grounds, no! It is because alcohol influences the center of perversion. And every religion is for meditation because meditation means creating a stillness more and more, becoming silent more and more.

Alcohol goes on doing quite the opposite—makes you more and more agitated, excited, disturbed. A trembling enters within you. The drunkard cannot even walk rightly; his balance is lost. Balance is lost not only in the body, but in the mind also.

Meditation means gaining the inner balance. When you gain the inner balance and there is no trembling, the whole body-mind has become still—then the center of right-knowledge starts functioning. Through that center, whatsoever is known is true.

Where are you? You are not alcoholics, you are not meditators; you must be somewhere between the two. You are not in any center. You are between these two centers of wrong-knowledge and right-knowledge. That's why you are confused.

Sometimes you have glimpses. You lean a little towards the right-knowledge center, then certain glimpses come to you. You lean toward the center which is of perversion, then perversion enters in you. And everything is mixed, you are in chaos. That's why either you will have to become meditators or you will have to become alcoholics, because confusion is too much and these are the two ways.

Either you lose yourself into intoxication: then you are at ease... at least you have gained a center—maybe of wrong-knowledge, but you are centered. The whole world may say you are wrong. You don't think so, you think the whole world is wrong. At least in those moments of unconsciousness you are centered, centered in the wrong center. But you are happy because even centering in the wrong center gives a certain happiness. You enjoy it, hence, so much appeal of alcohol.

Governments have been fighting for centuries. Laws have been made, prohibition and everything, but nothing helps. Unless humanity becomes meditative, nothing can help. People will go on—they will find new ways and new means to get intoxicated. They cannot be prevented, and the more you try to prevent them the more prohibition laws and the more appeal.

America did it and had to fall back. They tried their best, but when alcohol was prohibited more alcohol was used. They tried, they failed. India has been trying since Independence. It has failed, and many states have started again. It seems useless.

Unless man changes inwardly, you cannot force man by any prohibition; it is impossible, because then man will go mad. This is his way of remaining sane. For a few hours he becomes drugged, 'stoned', then he is okay. Then there is no misery, then there is no anguish. The misery will come, the anguish will come, but at least it is postponed. Tomorrow morning the misery will be there, the anguish will be there—he will have to face it. But by the evening he can hope again; he will take drink and be at ease.

These are the two alternatives. If you are not meditative then sooner or later you will have to find some drug. And there are subtle drugs. Alcohol is not very subtle, it is very gross. There are subtle drugs. Sex may become a drug for you. And through sex you may be just losing your consciousness. You can use anything as a drug. Only meditation can help. Why?—because meditation gives you centering on the center which Patanjali calls praman.

Why so much emphasis of every religion for meditation? Meditation must be doing some inner miracle. This is the miracle: that meditation helps you to put on the light of right-knowledge. Then wherever you move, then wherever your focus moves, whatsoever is known is true.

Buddha has been asked thousands and thousands of questions. One day somebody asked him, "We come with new questions. We have not even put the question before you and you start answering. You never think about it. How does it happen?"

So Buddha said, "It is not a question of thinking. You put the question and I simply look at it, and whatsoever is true is revealed. It is not a question of thinking and brooding about it. The answer is not coming as a logical syllogism. It is just a focusing of the right center."

Buddha is like a torch. Wherever the torch moves, it reveals. Whatsoever the question, that is not the point. Buddha has the light, and whenever that light will come on any question the answer will be revealed. The answer will come out of that light. It is a simple phenomenon, a revelation.

When somebody asks you, you have to think about it. But how can you think if you don't know? If you know there is no need to think. If you don't know what will you do? You will search in the memory, you will find out many clues. You will just do a patchwork. You don't really know, otherwise the response would have been immediate.

I have heard about one teacher, a woman teacher in a primary school. And she asked the children, "Have you got any questions?"

One small boy stood and he said, "I have one question and I have been waiting... whenever you ask I will ask it: what is the weight of the whole Earth?"

She became disturbed because she had never thought about it, never read about it. What is the weight of the whole Earth? So she played a trick teachers know. They have to play tricks. She said, "Yes, the question is significant. Now tomorrow, everybody has to find the answer." She needed time. "Tomorrow I will ask the question, and for whoever brings the right answer there will be a present for him."

All the children searched and searched, but they couldn't find. And the teacher ran to the library. The whole night she searched, and only just by the morning could she find out the weight of the Earth. She was very happy. She came back to school and the children were there. They were exhausted. They said they couldn't find the answer. "We asked Mom and we asked Dad and we asked everybody. Nobody knows. This question seems to be so difficult."

The teacher laughed and she said, "This is not difficult. I know the answer, but I was just trying to see whether you could find it out or not. This is the weight of the Earth...."

That small child who had raised the question, he stood again and he said, "With people or without?" Now the same situation....

You cannot put Buddha in such a situation. It is not a

question of finding somewhere; it is not really a question of answering you. Your question is just an excuse. When you put a question to Buddha, he simply moves his light towards that question and whatsoever is revealed is revealed. He answers you, that is a deep response of his right-center, praman.

Patanjali says there are five modifications of the mind. Right-knowledge: if this center of right-knowledge starts functioning in you, you will become a sage, a saint. You will become religious. Before that you cannot become religious.

That's why Jesus or Mohammed, they look mad—because they don't argue; they don't put their case logically, they simply assert. You ask Jesus, "Are you really the only son of God?" He says, "Yes." And if you ask him, "Prove it," he will laugh. He will say, "There is no need to prove. I know. This is the case, this is self-evident." To us it looks illogical. This man seems to be neurotic, claiming something without any proof.

If this praman, this center of prama, this center of right-knowledge starts functioning, you will be the same: you can assert but you cannot prove. How can you prove? If you are in love how can you prove that you are in love? You can simply assert. You have a pain in your leg: how can you prove that you have pain? You simply assert, "I have pain." You know somewhere inside; that knowing is enough.

Ramakrishna was asked, "Is there a God?"

He said "Yes."

He was asked, "Then prove it."

He said, "There is no need—I know. For me there is no need. For you there is a need, so you search. Nobody could prove it for me, I cannot prove it for you. I had to seek, I had to find. And I have found God is!"

This is the functioning of the right center. So Ramakrishna or Jesus look absurd: they are claiming certain things without giving any proof. They are not claiming, they are not claiming anything. Certain things are revealed to them because they have a new center functioning which you don't have—and because you don't have it you have to prove.

Remember, proving proves that you don't have an inner feeling of anything, everything has to be proved—even love has to be proved. And people go on....

I know many couples: the husband goes on proving that he loves and he has not convinced the wife, and the wife goes on proving that she loves and she has not convinced the husband. They remain unconvinced and that remains the conflict. And they go on feeling that the other has not yet proved it. Lovers go on searching. They create situations in which you have to prove that you love. And by and by both get bored—this futile effort to prove and nothing can be proved.

How can you prove love? You can give presents, but nothing is proved. You can kiss and hug and you can sing, you can dance, but nothing is proved. You may be just pretending.

This first modification of the mind is right-knowledge. Meditation leads to this modification. And when you can know rightly and there is no need to prove, only then mind can be dropped, not before it. When there is no need to prove mind is not needed, because mind is a logical instrument. You need it every moment. You have to think, find out what is wrong and what is right. Every moment there are choices and alternatives. You have to choose.

Only when praman functions, when right-knowledge functions, can you drop the mind, because now choosing has no meaning. You move choicelessly; whatsoever is right is revealed to you.

The definition of a sage is: one who never chooses. He never chooses good against bad. He simply moves towards the direction which is that of good. It is just like sunflowers: when the sun is in the east the flower turns to the east, it never chooses; when the sun moves to the west the flower turns to the west. It simply moves with the sun. It has not chosen to move, it has not decided; it has not taken a decision, "Now I should move because the sun has moved to the west."

A sage is just like a sunflower—he simply moves wherever good is. So whatsoever he does is good. The Upanishads say, "Don't judge sages. Your ordinary measurements won't do." You have to do good against bad. He has nothing to choose, he simply moves; whatsoever he does is good. And you cannot change him because it is not a question of alternatives. If you say, "This is bad," he will say, "Okay, it may be bad, but this is how I move, this is how my being flows."

Those who knew—and people in the days of the Upanishads knew—have decided that, "We will not judge a sage." Once a person has come to be centered in himself, when a person has achieved meditation, once a person has become silent and the mind has been dropped, he is beyond our morality, beyond tradition. He is beyond our limitations. If we can follow we can follow him; if we cannot follow we are helpless. But nothing can be done and we should not judge.

If right-knowledge functions, if your mind has taken the modification of right-knowledge, you will become religious. Look, it is totally different. Patanjali doesn't say if you go to the mosque, to the gurudwara, to the temple, if you do some ritual, you pray.... No, that's not religion. You have to make your right-knowledge center function, so whether you go to the temple or not it is immaterial; it doesn't matter. If your right-knowledge center functions whatsoever you do is prayer and wherever you go is a temple.

Kabir has said, "Wherever I go I find you, my God. Wherever I move, I move into you, I stumble upon you. And whatsoever I do, even walking, eating, it is prayer." Kabir says, "This spontaneity is my samadhi. Just to be spontaneous is my meditation."

Second is wrong-knowledge: if your center of wrong-knowledge is functioning, then whatsoever you do you will do wrongly, and whatsoever you choose you will choose wrongly. Whatsoever you decide will be wrong because you are not deciding, the wrong center is functioning.

There are people: they feel very unfortunate because whatsoever they do goes wrong. And they try not to do wrong again, but that's not going to help because their center has to be changed. Their mind functions in a wrong way. They may think that they are doing good but they will do bad. With all their good wishes they cannot help it; they are helpless.

Mulla Nasruddin used to visit a saint. He visited for many, many days. And the saint was a silent one, he would not speak anything. Then Mulla Nasruddin had to ask; he said, "I have been coming again and again, waiting that you will say something. And you have not said anything. And unless you speak I cannot understand. So just give me a message for my life, a direction so I can move in that direction."

So that Sufi sage said, "Neki kar kuyen may dal": Do good, and throw it in the well. It is one of the oldest Sufi sayings: "Do good, and throw it in the well." It means do good and forget it immediately; don't carry it that, "I have done good."

So next day Mulla Nasruddin helped one old woman to cross the road, and then he pushed her into the well.

Neki kar kuyen may dal: Do good, and throw it in the well.

If your wrong center is functioning, whatsoever you do—you can read the Koran, you can read the Gita, and you will find meanings. Krishna would be shocked, Mohammed would be shocked to see that you could find such meanings.

Mahatma Gandhi wrote his autobiography with the intention that it would help people. Then many letters came to him because he describes his sex life. He was honest, one of the most honest men, so he wrote everything, whatsoever had happened in his past: how he was too much indulgent the day his father was dying; he couldn't sit by his father's side even that day, he had to go with his wife to bed.

And doctors had said, "This is the last night. Your father cannot survive till the morning. He will be dead by the morning." But just about twelve or one in the night he started feeling desire, sexual desire. The father was feeling sleepy so he slipped away, went to his wife and indulged in sex. And the wife was pregnant, it was the ninth month. And the father was dying, the father died in the night, and the child also died the moment he was born. So his whole life Gandhi had a deep repentance that he couldn't be with his dying father because sex was so obsessive.

So he wrote everything, he was honest—and just to help others. But many letters started coming to him, and those letters were such that he was shocked. Many people wrote to him, "Your autobiography is such that we have become more sexual than before reading it. Just reading through your autobiography we have become more sexual and indulgent. It is erotic."

If the wrong center is functioning then nothing can be done. Whatsoever you do, read, behave, it will be wrong. You will move to the wrong. You have a center which is forcing you to move towards the wrong. You can go to Buddha, but you will see something wrong in him immediately. You cannot meet Buddha— immediately you will see something wrong. You have a focusing for the wrong, a deep urge to find wrong anywhere, everywhere.

Patanjali calls this modification of the mind viparyaya. Viparyaya means perversion. You pervert everything. You interpret everything in such a way that it becomes a perversion.

Omar Khayyam writes, "I have heard that God is compassionate." This is beautiful. Mohammedans go on repeating, "God is rahman, compassion; rahim, compassion." They go on repeating, continuously. So Omar Khayyam says, "If he is really compassionate, if he is compassion, then there is no need to be afraid. I can go on committing sin. If he is compassion then what is the fear? I can commit whatsoever sin I want and he is compassion—so whenever I stand before him I will say, 'Rahim, rahman': Oh God of compassion, I have sinned.... But you are compassion; if you are really compassion then have compassion on me." So he goes on drinking, he goes on committing whatsoever he thinks is sin. He has interpreted in a very perverted way.

All over the world people have done that. In India we say, "If you go to the Ganges, if you bathe in the Ganges, your sins will dissolve." It was a beautiful concept in itself. It shows many things. It shows that sin is not something very deep, it is just like dust on you. So don't get too much obsessed by it, don't feel guilty; it is just dust and inside you remain pure. Even bathing in the Ganges can help. This is just to show you not to become so much obsessed with sin as Christianity has become. Guilt has become so burdensome, so even just taking a bath in the Ganges will help. Don't be so much afraid. But how have we interpreted it? We say, "Then it is okay—go on committing sin." And after a while, when you feel that now you have committed many sins, so give a chance to the Ganges to purify them and then come back and commit again. This is the center of perversion.

Third is imagination: mind has the faculty to imagine. It is good, it is beautiful. All that is beautiful has come through imagination. Paintings, art, dance, music, everything that is beautiful has come through the imagination. But everything that is ugly, that has also come through the imagination. Hitler, Mao, Mussolini, they have all come through imagination.

Hitler imagined a world of supermen. And he believed in Friedrich Nietzsche who had said, "Destroy all those who are weak. Destroy all those who are not super; leave only supermen on the Earth." So he destroyed. Just imagination, just utopian imagination—that just by destroying the weak, just by destroying the ugly, just by destroying the physically crippled you will have a beautiful world. But the very destruction is the most ugly thing possible in the world—the very destruction.

But he was working through imagination. He had an imagination, a utopian imagination—the most imaginative man! Hitler is one of the most imaginative, and his imagination became so fantastic and so mad that for his imagined world he tried to destroy this world completely. His imagination had gone mad.

Imagination can give you poetry and painting and art, and imagination can give you madness also. It depends how you use it. All the great scientific discoveries have been through imagination—people who could imagine, who could imagine the impossible. Now we can fly into the air, now we can go to the moon. These are deep imaginings.

Man has been imagining for centuries, millennia, how to fly, how to go to the moon. Every child is born with the desire to go to the moon, to catch the moon. But we reached it! Through imagination creativity comes, but through imagination destruction also comes.

Patanjali says, imagination is the third mode of mind. You can use it in a wrong way and then it will destroy you. You can also use it in a right way. And then there are imaginative meditations: they start with imagination, but by and by imagination becomes subtler and subtler and subtler. And then imagination is ultimately dropped and you are face to face with the truth.

All Christian and Mohammedan meditations are basically through imagination. First you have to imagine something, then you go on imagining it and then through imagination you create an atmosphere around you. You try it; try what is possible through imagination. Even the impossible is possible.

If you think you are beautiful, if you imagine you are beautiful, a certain beauty will start happening to your body. So whenever a man says to a woman, "You are beautiful," the woman changes immediately. She may not have been beautiful before this moment. She may not have been beautiful, just homely, ordinary, but this man has given imagination to her.

So every woman who is loved becomes more beautiful, every man who is loved becomes more beautiful. A person who is not loved may be beautiful, but becomes ugly because he cannot imagine, she cannot imagine. And if imagination is not there, you shrink.

Coue, one of the great psychologists of the West, helped millions of people to be cured of many, many diseases just through imagination. His formula was very simple. He would say, "You just start feeling that you are okay. Just go on repeating inside the mind, 'I am getting better and better. Every day I am getting better.' In the night, while you fall asleep, go on thinking you are healthy, and you are getting healthier every moment, and by the morning you will be the healthiest person in the world. Go on imagining."

And he helped millions of people. Even incurable diseases were cured. It looked like a miracle. It is nothing, it is just a basic law: your mind follows imagination.

Now psychologists say that if you say to children, "You are duffers, dull," they become dull. You force them to be dull. You give their imagination the suggestion that they are dull.

Many experiments have been done. Say to a child, "You are dull. You cannot do anything; you cannot solve this mathematical problem," and give him the problem and tell him, "Now try"— he will not be able to solve it. You have closed the door. Say to the child, "You are intelligent and I have not seen any boy as intelligent as you; for your stage, for your age you are over-intelligent. You show many potentialities, you can solve any problem. Now try this"—and he will be able to solve it. You have given imagination to him.

Now these are scientifically proved, scientifically discovered, that whatsoever imagination catches becomes a seed. Whole generations have been changed, whole ages, whole countries have been changed just through imagination.

You go to the Punjab…. I was traveling once from Delhi to Manali. My driver was a Sikh, a sardar. The way, the road, was dangerous, and the car was very big. And many times the driver became afraid. Many times he would say, "Now I cannot go ahead. We will have to go back."

We tried in every way to persuade him. At one point he became so afraid he stopped the car, got out of the car and said, "No! Now I cannot move from here. It is dangerous." He said. "It may not be dangerous for you, you may be ready to die. But I am not, I want to go back."

By chance one of my friends who is also a sardar and was a big police official was also coming. He was following me to attend the camp in Manali. His car arrived so I told him, "Do something! The man has got out of the car."

That police official came and he said, "You are a sardar, a Sikh, and a coward? Get into the car!"

The man immediately came into the car and started it. So I asked him, "What is the matter?"

He said, "Now he has touched my ego. He says, 'You are a sardar?'—'sardar' means leader of men—'a Sikh and a coward!' He has touched my imagination. He has touched my pride. Now we can go. Dead or alive, but we will reach Manali!"

And this has not happened with one man. If you go to the Punjab... it has happened with millions. Look at the Hindus of the Punjab and at the Sikhs of the Punjab. Their blood is the same, they belong to the same race. Just five hundred years ago all were Hindus. And then a different type of race, a military race, was born. Just by growing a beard, just by changing your face, you cannot become brave. But you can!... imagination. Nanak gave them the imagination that, "You are a different type of race. You are unconquerable." And once they believed, once that imagination started to work, within five hundred years a new race, totally different from Punjabi Hindus, has come into being in the Punjab. Nothing is different, but in India no one is braver than they. These two world wars have proved that on the whole of the Earth, Sikhs have no comparison. They can fight fearlessly.

What has happened? Just their imagination has created a milieu around them. They feel that just by being Sikhs they are different. Imagination works! It can make a brave man out of you, it can make you a coward.

I have heard: Mulla Nasruddin was sitting in a pub, drinking. He was not a brave man, one of the most cowardly—but alcohol gave him courage. And then a man, a giant of a man, entered the pub—ferocious looking, dangerous, looked like a murderer. At any other time, in his senses, Mulla Nasruddin would have been afraid, but now he was drunk so he was not afraid at all.

That ferocious looking man went near to Mulla, and seeing that he was not afraid at all he stomped on his feet. Mulla got angry, furious, and he said, "What are you doing? Are you doing it on purpose or is it just a sort of joke?" But by this time, by stomping on his feet, Mulla was brought back from his alcohol. He was brought back, he came to his senses. But he had said, "What are you doing? Is it on purpose or is it just a sort of joke?"

The man said, "On purpose."

Mulla Nasruddin said, "Then thank you. On purpose it is okay, because I don't like these types of jokes"

Patanjali says imagination is the third faculty. You go on imagining.... If you wrongly imagine you can create delusions around you, illusions, dreams—you can be lost in them. LSD and other drugs, they help and work on this center. So whatsoever potentiality you have inside, your LSD trip will help you develop it. So nothing is certain. If you have happy imaginations, the drug trip will be a happy trip, a high. If you have miserable imaginations, nightmarish imaginations, the trip is going to be bad.

That's why many people make contradictory reports. Huxley says it can become a key to the door of heaven, and Rheiner says it is ultimate hell. It depends on you; LSD cannot do anything. It simply jumps on your center of imagination and starts functioning there chemically. If you have an imagination of the nightmarish type then you will develop that, and you will pass through hell. And if you are addicted to beautiful dreams you may reach heaven.

This imagination can function either as a hell or as heaven. You can use it to go completely insane. What has happened to madmen in the madhouses? They have used their imagination, and they have used it in such a way that they are engulfed by it. A madman may be sitting alone and he is talking loudly to someone. He not only talks, he answers also. He questions, he answers, he speaks for the other who is absent also. You may think that he is mad, but he is talking to a real person. In his imagination the person is real, and he cannot judge what is imaginary and what is real.

Children cannot judge. So many times children may lose their toy in a dream, and then they will weep in the morning, "Where is my toy?" They cannot judge that a dream is a dream and reality is reality. And they have not lost anything, they were just dreaming. The boundaries are blurred; they don't know where the dream ends and where reality starts.

A madman is also blurred. He doesn't know what is real, what is unreal. If imagination is used rightly then you will know that this is imagination, and you will remain alert that this is imagination. You can enjoy it, but this is not real.

So when people meditate, many things happen through their

imagination. They start seeing lights, colors, visions, talking to God himself, or moving with Jesus or dancing with Krishna. These are imaginative things, and a meditator has to remember that these are functions of the imagination. You can enjoy it, nothing is wrong in them, they are fun——but don't think that they are real.

The fourth is sleep. Sleep means unconsciousness as far as your outward-moving consciousness is concerned. It has gone deep into itself. Activity has stopped, conscious activity has stopped. Mind is not functioning. Sleep is a non-functioning of the mind. If you are dreaming then it is not sleep. You are just in the middle between waking and sleep. You have left waking and you have not entered sleep; you are just in the middle.

Sleep means a totally contentless state——no activity, no movement in the mind. Mind has been completely absorbed, relaxed. This sleep is beautiful, it is life-giving. You can use it. And this sleep, if you know how to use it, can become samadhi. Because samadhi and sleep are not very different. There is only one difference: that in samadhi you will be aware; everything else will be the same.

In sleep everything is the same, only you are not aware. You are into the same bliss in which Buddha-entered, in which Ramakrishna lives, in which Jesus has made his home. In deep sleep you are in the same blissful state——but you are not aware. So in the morning you feel the night has been good, in the morning you feel refreshed, vital, rejuvenated. In the morning you feel that the night was just beautiful, but this is just an afterglow. You don't know what has happened, what really happened. You were not aware.

Sleep can be used in two ways. Just as a natural rest... you have even lost that. People are not really going into sleep——they go on dreaming continuously. Sometimes, for a very few seconds, they touch... they touch and they again start dreaming. The silence of sleep, the blissful music of sleep, has become unknown. You have destroyed it. Even natural sleep is destroyed. You are so agitated and excited that the mind cannot fall completely into oblivion.

But Patanjali says natural sleep is good for the body's health, and if you can become alert in sleep it can become samadhi, it can become a spiritual phenomenon. So there are techniques——we will discuss them later on——of how sleep can become an awakening. The Gita says that the yogi doesn't sleep even while he is asleep. He remains alert, something inside goes on being aware. The whole body falls into sleep, the mind falls into sleep, but the witnessing remains. Someone is watching——a watcher on the tower goes on. Then sleep becomes samadhi; it becomes the ultimate ecstasy.

And the last is memory. Memory is the fifth modification of the mind. That too can be used or misused. If memory is misused it creates confusion. Really, you may remember something, but you cannot be certain whether it happened that way or not. Your memory is not reliable. You may add many things to it; imagination may enter into it. You may delete many things from it, you may do many things to it. And when you say, "This is my memory," it is a very refined and changed thing. It is not real.

Everybody says, "My childhood was just paradise"——and look at children. These children will also say later on that their childhood was paradise... and they are suffering. And every child hankers to grow up soon, how to become an adult. Every child thinks that adults are enjoying, they are enjoying all that is worth enjoying. They are powerful, they can do everything; he is helpless. Children think they are suffering. But these children will grow as you have grown, and then later on they will say that childhood was beautiful, just a paradise.

Your memory is not reliable. You are imagining. You are just creating your past. You are not true to it. And you drop many things from it—you drop all that was ugly, all that was sad, all that was painful; all that was beautiful you continue. You remember all that was a support to your ego, and all that was not a support you drop it, you forget it.

So everybody has a great storehouse of dropped memories. And whatsoever you say is not true you cannot remember truly. All your centers are confused and they enter into each other and disturb.

Right-memory... Buddha has used the words 'right-memory' for meditation. Patanjali says, if memory is right, that means one has to be totally honest with oneself. Then, only then, can memory be right. Whatsoever has happened, bad or good, don't change it. Know it as it is. It is very hard. It is arduous. You choose and change. Knowing one's past as it is will change your whole life. If you rightly know your past as it is, you will not like to repeat it in the future. Right now everybody is thinking of how to repeat it in a modified form, but if you know your past exactly as it was you will not like to repeat it.

Right-memory will give you the impetus of how to be free from all lives. And if memory is right then you can even go into past lives. If you are honest then you can go into past lives. And then you have only one desire: how to transcend all this nonsense. But you think the past was beautiful, and you think the future is going to be beautiful, only this present is wrong. But the past was present a few days before, and the future will become present a few days after. And each time each present is wrong and all past is beautiful and all future is beautiful. This is wrong memory. Look directly, don't change. Look at the past as it was. But we are dishonest....

Every man hates his father, but if you ask anybody he will say, "I love my father. I honor my father as no one else." Every woman hates her mother, but ask and every woman will say, "My mother, she is just divine." This is wrong-memory.

Gibran has a story. He says, one night a mother and daughter were awakened suddenly because of a noise. They both were sleepwalkers, and at the time the sudden noise happened in the neighborhood, they were both walking in the garden, asleep. They were sleepwalkers.

It must have been a shock, because in sleep the old woman, the mother, was saying to the daughter, "Because of you, you bitch—because of you my youth is lost. You destroyed me. And now anybody who comes to the house looks at you. Nobody looks at me." A deep jealousy that comes to every mother when the daughter becomes young and beautiful: it happens to every mother, but it is inside.

And the daughter was saying, "You old rotten.... Because of you I cannot enjoy life. You are the hindrance. Everywhere you are the hindrance, the obstacle. I cannot love, I cannot enjoy."

And suddenly, because of the noise, they were both awakened. And the old woman said, "My child, what are you doing here? You may catch cold. Come inside."

And the daughter said, "But what are you doing here? You were not feeling well and this is a cold night. Come, mother. Come to bed."

The first thing that was happening was coming from the unconscious. Now they are again pretending. They have become awake. Now the unconscious has gone back, the conscious mind has come in. Now they are hypocrites. Your conscious mind is hypocrisy.

To be truly honest with one's own memories one will have to really pass through arduous effort. And you have to be true, whatsoever it is. You have to be nakedly true. You have to know what you really think about your father, about your mother, about your brother, about your sister—really. And don't mix, don't change, don't polish what you have in the past; let it be as it is. If this happens, then, Patanjali says, this will be a freedom. You will drop it. The whole thing is nonsense and you will not like to project it again into the future.

And then you will not be a hypocrite. You will be real, true, sincere. You will become authentic. And when you become authentic you become like a rock: nothing can change you, nothing can create confusion.

You become like a sword: you can always cut whatsoever is wrong, you can divide whatsoever is right from the wrong. And then a clarity of mind is achieved. That clarity can lead you towards meditation. That clarity can become the basic ground to grow—to grow beyond.

Enough for today?

4

MADNESS
OR MEDITATION

see a real flower. Just by hearing "This is a rose" you say "Beautiful!" mechanically. You have not felt the beauty, you have not sensed the beauty, you have not touched this flower. Just "rose is beautiful" is in your mind, the moment you hear 'rose' the mind projects and says "It is beautiful."

And you may believe that you have come to feel that the rose is beautiful, this is not so. This is false. Just look. That's why children come to things more deeply than grown-up people, because they don't know names. They are not yet prejudiced. If a rose is beautiful only then will it be beautiful, all roses are not beautiful. Children come near to things, their eyes are fresh. They see things as they are because they don't know how to project anything.

The first question:
You said that there are only two
alternatives for men, either madness
or meditation. But millions of people
on the earth have not reached to
either of the two. Do you think
they will?

information. This is one of the most recent psychological findings, that children have more intelligence than when they leave the university. The latest findings prove this. When children enter in the first grade, they have more intelligence. They will have less and less intelligence as they grow in knowledge. And by the time they become bachelors and masters and doctors, they are finished. When they come back with a doctor's degree, a Ph.D., they have left their intelligence somewhere in the university. They are dead, filled with knowledge, crammed with knowledge—but this knowledge is just false, a prejudice about everything. Now they cannot feel things directly, they cannot feel live persons directly, they cannot live directly. Everything has become verbal, wordy. It is not real now, it has become mental.

Wrong knowledge is a false conception not corresponding to

They have reached! They have not reached to meditation, but they have reached to madness. And the difference between the mad who are in the madhouses and the mad who are outside is only of degrees. There is no qualitative difference, the difference is only of quantity. You may be less mad, they may be more mad, but man as he is is mad.

Why do I say man as he is is mad? Madness means many things. One, you are not centered. If you are not centered you will be insane. Not centered, many voices in you—you are many, you are a multitude. And no one is a master in the house, and every servant of the house claims to be the master. There is confusion, conflict and a continuous struggle. You are in a continuous civil war. If this civil war is not going on then you will be in meditation. It continues day and night, for twenty-four hours. Write down whatsoever goes on in your mind for a few minutes, and be honest. Write down exactly whatsoever goes on and you yourself will feel that this is mad.

I have a particular technique I use with many persons. I say to them, sit in a closed room and then start talking loudly, whatsoever comes in the mind. Talk loudly so that you can listen.

This fifteen minutes of talking, and you will feel that you are listening to a madman. Absurd, inconsistent, unrelated fragments float in the mind——and that is your mind! So you may be ninety-nine percent mad and someone else has crossed the boundary, he has gone beyond one hundred percent. Those who have gone beyond one hundred percent, we put them in the madhouses. We cannot put you in the madhouse because there are not so many madhouses. And there cannot be——then the whole Earth has to be a madhouse.

Khalil Gibran writes a small anecdote. He says one of his friends became mad so he was put in a madhouse. Then just out of love, compassion, he went to see him, to visit him. He was sitting under a tree in the garden of the madhouse, surrounded by a very big wall. Khalil Gibran went there, sat by the side with his friend on the bench and asked him, "Do you ever think about why you are here?"

The madman laughed and he said, "I am here because I wanted to leave that big madhouse outside. And I am at peace here. In this madhouse——you call it a madhouse——no one is mad."

Mad people cannot think that they are mad; that is one of the basic characteristics of madness. If you are mad you cannot think that you are mad. If you can think you are mad there is a possibility.... If you can think and conceive that you are mad you are still a little sane. The madness has not occurred in its totality. So this is the paradox: those who are really sane, they know that they are mad, and those who are completely mad, they cannot think that they are mad.

You never think that you are mad: that is part of madness. You are not centered; you cannot be sane. Your sanity is just superficial, arranged. Just on the surface you appear to be sane. That's why, continuously, you have to deceive the world around you. You have to hide much, you have to prevent much. You don't allow everything to come out. You are suppressive: you may be thinking something but you will say something else. You are pretending, and because of this pretension you can have the minimum superficial sanity around you; inside you are boiling.

Sometimes there are eruptions. In anger you erupt and the madness that you have been hiding comes out. It breaks all your adjustments. So psychologists say anger is a temporary madness. You will again regain balance, you will again hide your reality, you will again polish your surface——you will again become sane. And you will say that, "It was wrong. I did it in spite of myself. I never meant it, so forgive me." But you meant it! That was more real! This asking for forgiveness is just a pretension. Again you are maintaining your surface, your mask.

A sane man has no mask. His face is original: whatsoever he is, he is. A madman has to continuously change his faces. Every moment he has to use a different mask for a differ-ent situation, for different relationships. Just watch yourself changing your faces: when you come to your wife you have a different face, when you go to your beloved, your mistress, you have a totally different face. When you talk to your servant you have a different mask and when you talk to your master, a totally different face. It may be that your servant is standing on your right and your boss is standing on your left——then you have two faces simultaneously. On the left you have one face, on the right you have a different face. Because to the servant you cannot show the same face; you need not——you are the boss there, so one side of the face will be 'the boss'. You cannot show that 'boss face' to your boss, you are a servant there; your other side will show a servile attitude.

This is continuously going on. You are not watching, that's why you are not aware. If you watch you will become aware that you are mad. You don't have any face—or, the original face has been lost. To regain the original face is what meditation means.

So Zen masters say, "Go and find out your original face, the face you had before you were born, the face you will have when you have died." Between birth and death you have false faces. You continuously go on deceiving—and not only others: when you stand before a mirror you deceive yourself, you never see your real face in the mirror. You don't have that much courage to face yourself. That face in the mirror is also false. You create it, you enjoy it; it is a painted mask.

We are not only deceiving others, we are also deceiving ourselves. Really, we cannot deceive others if we have not already deceived ourselves. So we have to believe in our own lies, only then can we make others believe. If you don't believe in your lies nobody else is going to be deceived.

And this whole nuisance that you call your life leads nowhere. It is a mad affair. You work too much, you overwork; you walk and run. And the whole life you struggle and you reach nowhere. You don't know from where you are coming, you don't know where you are moving, to where you are going. If you meet a man on the road and you ask him, "Where are you coming from, sir?" and he says, "I don't know," and you ask him, "Where are you going," and he says, "I don't know," and still he says, "Don't prevent me, I am in a hurry," what will you think about him? You will think he is mad.

If you don't know where you are coming from and where you are going to, then what is the hurry? But this is the situation of everybody, and everybody is on the road. Life is a road—you are always in the middle—and you don't know where you have come from, you don't know where you are going. You have no knowledge of the source, no knowledge of the goal, but you are in a great hurry, making every effort to reach nowhere.

What type of sanity is this? And out of this whole struggle not even glimpses of happiness come to you—not even glimpses. You simply hope someday, somewhere, tomorrow, the day after tomorrow—or after death, in some afterlife—that happiness is waiting for you. This is just a trick just to postpone, just so as not to feel too miserable right now.

You don't even have glimpses of bliss. What type of sanity is this? Continuous misery—and over and above, that mis-ery is not created by anybody else. You create your suffering. What type of sanity is this? You create your suffering continuously! I call it madness.

Sanity will be this: you will become aware that you are not centered. So the first thing to be done is to be centered, to get centered—to have a center within yourself from where you can lead your life, from where you can discipline your life; to have a master within you from where you can direct, you can move. The first thing is to be crystallized, and then the second thing will be not to create suffering for yourself. Drop all that creates suffering, all those motives, desires, hopes which create suffering.

But you are not aware. You simply go on doing it, you don't see that you create it. Whatsoever you do, you are sowing some seeds. Then trees will follow, and whatsoever you have sown you will reap it. And whenever you reap anything there is suffering, but you never look that these seeds were sown by you Whenever suffering happens to you, you think it is coming from somewhere else. You think it is some accident or that some evil forces are working against you. So you have invented the Devil.

The Devil is just a scapegoat. You are the Devil; you create your suffering. But whenever you suffer you simply throw it on the Devil: "The Devil is doing something." Then you are at ease. Then you never become aware of your own foolish pattern of life, stupid pattern of life.

Or you call it fate, or you say, "God is testing me." But you go on avoiding the basic fact that you are the sole cause of whatsoever happens to you. And nothing is accidental. Everything has a causal link—and you are the cause.

For example, you fall in love. Love gives you a feeling, a feeling that bliss is somewhere nearby. You feel for the first time that you are welcomed by someone, at least one person welcomes you. You start flowering. Even one person welcoming you, waiting for you, loving you, caring for you, you start flowering. Just in the beginning… and then immediately your wrong patterns start working—you immediately want to possess the beloved, the loved one.

And possession is killing. The moment you possess the lover you have killed. Then you suffer. Then you weep and cry and you think that the lover is wrong, fate is wrong, "Destiny is not in my favor." But you don't know that you have poisoned love through possession, through possessiveness.

But every lover is doing that, and every lover suffers. Love, which can give you the deepest blessings, becomes the deepest misery. So old cultures, particularly in India in the old days, have completely destroyed the phenomenon of love. They had arranged marriages for children—no possibility of falling in love, because love leads to misery. This was such a known phenomenon that if you allow love, then love leads to misery, so it is better not to have the possibility. Let the children, small children, be married. Before they can fall in love let them be married. Then they will never know what love is and they will not be in misery.

But love never creates misery—it is you who poisons it. Love is always joy, love is always celebration. Love is the deepest ecstasy that nature allows you, but you destroy it. So just not to fall into misery, in India and in other old, ancient countries, the possibility of love was completely closed. So then you will not fall in misery—but then you have also missed the only ecstasy that nature allows. So a mediocre life will be there: no misery, no happiness, just going on somehow. This is what marriage has been in the past.

Now America is trying, the West is trying to revive love. But much misery is coming through that, and sooner or later Western countries will have to decide for child marriage again. A few psychologists have already proposed that child marriage has to be brought back because love is creating so much misery. But I again say, it is not love. Love cannot create misery. It is you, your pattern of madness which creates misery—and not only in love, everywhere. Everywhere you are bound to bring your mind.

For example, many people come to me. They start meditating. In the beginning there are sudden flashes, but only in the beginning. Once they have known certain experiences, once they have known certain glimpses, everything stops. And they come to me weeping and crying and they say, "What is happening? Something was going to happen, something was happening, now everything has stopped. And we are trying our best, but nothing, nothing comes out of it."

I tell them, "It happened for the first time because you were not expecting. Now you are expecting so the whole situation has changed. When you ha : that feeling of weightlessness for the first time, a feeling of being f led by something unknown, a feeling of being carried from your dead life, a feeling of ecstatic moments, you were not expecting it. You had never known such moments. For the first time they were falling on you. You were unaware, unexpecting. That was the situation.

"Now you are changing the situation. Now every day you sit for meditation and you are expecting. Now you are cunning, clever, calculating. When you had the glimpse for the first time you were innocent, just like a child. You were playing with meditation, but there was no expectation. Then it happened. It will happen again, but then you will have to again be innocent.

"Now your mind is bringing you misery, and if you go on insisting that, 'I must have the experience again and again,' you will lose it forever. Unless you forget it completely, it may take years. Unless you become again completely inattentive that somewhere in the past there was such a happening, only then will the possibility again be open to you."

This I call madness: you destroy everything. Whatsoever comes in your hand, you immediately destroy it. And remember, life gives you many gifts, unasked. You have never asked life, and life gives you many gifts. But you destroy every gift and every gift can become greater and greater. It can grow because life never gives you anything dead. If love has been given to you, it can grow. It can grow to unknown dimensions, but the very first moment you destroy it.

If meditation has happened to you, just feel thankful to the divine and forget it. Just feel grateful, and remember well that you don't have any capacity to have it, you are not in any way authorized to have it; it has been a gift. It has been an overflowing of the divine. Forget it. Don't expect it, don't demand it. It will come next day again—deeper, higher, greater. It will go on expanding, but every day drop it from the mind.

There is no end to its possibilities. It will become infinite; the whole cosmos will become ecstatic for you. But your mind has to be dropped. Your mind is the madness. So when I say there are only two alternatives, madness and meditation, I mean mind and meditation. If you remain confined in the mind you will remain mad. Unless you transcend the mind you cannot transcend madness. At the most you can be a functioning member of the society, that's all. And you can be a functioning member of the society because the whole society is just like you. Everybody is mad, so madness is the rule.

Become aware—and don't think that others are mad; feel it deeply that you are mad and something has to be done. Immediately! It is an emergency! Don't postpone it because there may come a moment when you cannot do anything. You may go so mad that you cannot do anything.

Right now you can do something. You are still within limits. Something can be done, some efforts can be made; the pattern can be changed. But a moment can come when you cannot do anything, when you have become completely shattered and you have lost even the consciousness.

If you can feel that you are mad this is a very hopeful sign. It shows you can become alert towards your own reality. The door is there, you can become really sane. At least this much sanity is there—that you can understand.

The second question:

Capacity of right-knowledge is one of the five faculties of the mind, but it is not a state of no-mind. Then how is it possible that whatsoever one sees through this center is true? Does this center of right-knowledge function after enlightenment, or can even a meditator, a sadhak, be with this center?

Yes, the center of right-knowledge, praman, is still within the mind. Ignorance is of the mind, knowledge is also of the mind. When you go beyond mind there is neither; there is neither ignorance nor knowledge. Knowledge is also a disease. It is a good disease, a golden one, but it is a disease. So really, it cannot be said that Buddha knows, it cannot be said that he doesn't know. He has gone beyond. Whether he knows or is ignorant, nothing can be asserted about it.

When there is no mind, how can you know or not know? Knowing is through mind, not knowing is also through mind. Through mind you can know wrongly, through mind you can know rightly. When there is no mind, knowledge and ignorance both cease. This will be difficult to understand, but it is easy if you follow: mind knows, so mind can be ignorant; when there is no mind how can you be ignorant and how can you be knowing? You are, but knowing and not knowing, both have ceased.

Mind has two centers: one, of right-knowledge. If that center functions it starts functioning through concentration, meditation, contemplation, prayer—then whatsoever you know is true. There is a wrong center: it functions if you are sleepy, live in a hypnotic-like state, intoxicated with something or other—sex, music, drugs or anything.

You can be addicted to food, then it becomes an intoxicant.

You may be eating too much. You are mad, obsessed, with food. Then food becomes like alcohol. Anything that takes possession of your mind, anything without which you cannot live, it becomes intoxicating. So if you live through intoxicants then your center of wrong-knowledge functions and whatsoever you know is false, untrue. You live in a world of lies.

But both these centers belong to the mind. When mind drops and meditation has come to its totality.... In Sanskrit we have two terms: one term is dhyana—dhyana means meditation; and the other term is samadhi. Samadhi means perfect meditation, where even meditation has become unnecessary, where even to do meditation is meaningless. You cannot do it, you have become it—then it is samadhi.

In this state of samadhi there is no mind. And there is neither knowledge nor ignorance, there is only pure being. This pure being is a totally different dimension. It is not a dimension of knowing, it is a dimension of being.

Even if such a man, a Buddha or a Jesus, wants to communicate to you, he will have to use mind. For communication he will have to use mind. And if you ask a certain question he will have to use his center of mind for right-knowledge. Mind is the instrument of communication, of thinking, of knowing.

But when you are not asking anything and Buddha is sitting under his bo tree, he is neither ignorant nor a knower. He is there. Really, there is no difference between the tree and the Buddha. There is a difference, but in a way there is no difference. He has become just as if a tree; he just exists. There is no movement, even of knowledge. The sun will rise but he will not know that the sun has risen. Not that he will remain ignorant——no, simply that is now not his movement. He has become so silent, so still, that

117

nothing moves. He is just like the tree. The tree is totally ignorant. Or, you can say the tree is just below the mind; the mind has not started functioning. The tree will become man in some life, the tree will become mad like you in some life...and the tree will try for meditation in some life, and the tree will also one day become a buddha. The tree is below mind, and Buddha sitting under the tree is beyond mind. They both are mindless. One is still to attain the mind and one has attained and crossed over it.

So when mind is transcended, when no-mind is achieved, you are a pure being, satchitananda. There is no happening in you. Neither is there action nor is there knowing—but it is difficult for us....

Scriptures go on saying that all duality is transcended. Knowledge is also part of duality—ignorance, knowledge. But so-called saints go on saying that Buddha had become 'a knower'. Then we are clinging to the duality. That's why Buddha never answered. Many times, millions of times it had been asked of him, "What happens when a person becomes a buddha?" He remained silent. He said, "Become and know." Nothing can be said about what happens because whatsoever can be said will be said in your language. And your language is basically dualistic so whatsoever can be said will be untrue.

If it is said that he knows it will be untrue, if it is said that he has become immortal it will be untrue, if it is said that now he has achieved bliss it will be untrue—because all duality disappears. Misery disappears, happiness disappears. Ignorance disappears, knowledge disappears. Darkness disappears, light disappears. Death disappears, life disappears. Nothing can be said. Or, only this much can be said—that whatsoever you can think will not be there, whatsoever you can conceive of will not be there. And the only way is, to become that. Then only do you know.

The third question:
You said that if we see visions of Rama or that we are dancing with Krishna, to remember it is only imagination. But the other night you said that if we were receptive we could communicate with Christ, Buddha or Krishna right now. Is that communication also imagination when it happens; or are there meditative states in which Christ or Buddha are really there?

A little difficult to be understood....

The first thing: out of one hundred cases, ninety-nine cases will be of imagination. You imagine: that's why to a Christian Krishna never appears in visions; to a Hindu Mohammed never appears in his visions. Leave Mohammed and Jesus; they are far away. But to a Jaina Rama never appears in his visions—cannot appear. To a Hindu Mahavira never appears. Why?—you don't have any imagination for Mahavira.

If you are born a Hindu you have been fed with the concept of Rama and Krishna. If you are born a Christian you have been fed—your computer, your mind, has been fed—with the image of Jesus. Whenever you start meditating that fed-in image comes up in the mind; it flashes in the mind.

Jesus appears to you, Jesus never appears to Jews. And he was a Jew. He was born a Jew, he died a Jew, but he never appears to Jews because they never believed in him. They thought he was just a vagabond, they crucified him as a criminal. Jesus never appears to Jews; he belonged to Jews, he had Jewish blood and bones.

I have heard a joke that in Nazi Germany soldiers of Hitler

were killing Jews in a town. They had killed many. A few Jews escaped. It was a Sunday morning. They escaped; they went into a church because they thought that would be the best hiding place, the Christian church. The church was filled with Christians, it was a Sunday morning. So a few, a dozen Jews were hiding there.

But the soldiers got the news that some Jews had gone into the church and they were hiding there. So they went into the church; they told the priest, "Stop your services!" The leader of the soldiers went to the rostrum and said, "You cannot deceive us. There are a few Jews hiding here. So anyone who is a Jew should go out and stand in a line. If you follow our orders you can save yourself. If someone tries to deceive, he will be killed immediately."

So by and by, the Jews came out of the church and they stood in a line. Then suddenly the whole crowd in the church became aware that Jesus had disappeared, the statue of Jesus. He was also a Jew so he was standing outside in the line!

But Jesus never appears to Jews. He was not a Christian, he never belonged to any Christian church. If he comes back he will not recognize a Christian church, he will go to the synagogue; he will go to the Jewish community. He will go to see the rabbi, he cannot go to see a Catholic or Protestant priest. He doesn't know. But he never appears to Jews because he has never been a seed in their imagination. They refused him, so the seed is not there.

So whatsoever happens, ninety-nine possibilities are that it may be just fed-in knowledge, concepts, images: they flash before your mind. And when you start meditating you become sensitive. You become so sensitive that you can become a victim of your own imagination. And the imagination will look so real, and there is no way to judge whether it is real or unreal.

Only in one percent of cases will it not be imaginary, but how to know? In that one percent of cases there will be no image, really. You will not feel Jesus standing before you crucified, you will not feel Krishna standing before you and you dancing with him. You will feel the presence but there will be no image, remember this. You will feel a descendance of divine presence. You will be filled with something unknown, but without any form. There will be no dancing Krishna and there will be no crucified Jesus and there will be no Buddha sitting in siddhasan, no! There will simply be a presence, a vital presence that is flowing within you, in and out. You are overwhelmed, you are in the ocean of it.

Jesus will not be within you, you will be in Jesus; that will be the difference. Krishna will not be in your mind, an image; you will be in Krishna. But then Krishna will be formless. It will be an experience but not an image.

Then why call it Krishna? There will be no form. Why call it Jesus? These are simply symbols, linguistic symbols. You are acquainted with the word 'Jesus' so when that presence fills you and you become part of it, a vibrating part of it, when you become a drop in that ocean, how to express it? You know the most beautiful word for you may be 'Jesus' or the most beautiful word may be 'Buddha' or 'Krishna'—these words are fed into the mind so you have to choose these certain words to indicate toward that presence.

But that presence is not an image, it is not a dream. It is not a vision at all. You can use Jesus, you can use Krishna, you can use Christ, or whatsoever—whatsoever name has appeal for you, whatsoever name has a love-appeal for you, that's up to you.

That word and that name and that image will come from your mind, but the experience itself is imageless. It is not an imagination.

One Catholic priest was visiting a Zen master, Nan-in. Nan-in had never heard about Jesus, so this Catholic priest thought, "It will be good. I should go and read some parts from The Sermon on the Mount, and I will see how Nan-in reacts. And people say that he is enlightened."

So that Catholic priest went to Nan-in and he said, "Master, I am a Christian, and I have got a book and I love it. I would like to read something from it just to know how you respond, how you react." So he read a few lines from The Sermon on the Mount, The New Testament. He translated it into Japanese because Nan-in could understand only Japanese.

When he started translating, the whole face of Nan-in changed completely. Tears started flowing from his eyes and he said, "These are the words of Buddha."

The Christian priest said, "No, no, these are the words of Jesus."

But Nan-in said, "Whatsoever name you give, I feel these are the words of the Buddha, because I know only Buddha and these words can come only through Buddha. And if you say they have come through Jesus, then Jesus was a buddha; that doesn't make any difference. Then I will tell my disciples that Jesus was a Buddhist."

This will be the feeling. If you feel the presence of the divine, then names are just immaterial. Names are bound to be different for everyone because names come from education, names come from culture, names come from the race you belong to. But that experience doesn't belong to any society, that experience doesn't

122

belong to any culture, that experience doesn't belong to your mind, the computer—it belongs to you.

So remember, if you see visions, they are imagination. If you start feeling presences, formless, existential experiences—enveloped in them, merged in them, melting in them—then you are really in contact.

You can call that presence Jesus, you can call that presence Buddha, it depends on you; it makes no difference. Jesus is a buddha and Buddha is a christ. Those who have gone beyond the mind, they have also gone beyond personalities. They have also gone beyond forms. If Jesus and Buddha are standing together, there will be two bodies but one soul. There will be two bodies but not two presences... one presence.

It is just like if you put two lamps in a room. The lamps are two, just their bodies, but the light has become one. You cannot demarcate that this light belongs to this lamp and that light belongs to that lamp. The lights have merged. Only the material part of the lamp has remained separate, but the non-material part has become one.

If Buddha and Jesus come close, if they stand together, you will see two lamps, separate, but their lights have already merged. They have become one. All those who have known truth have become one. Their names are different for their followers; for them, now there are no names.

The fourth question:

Please explain whether awareness is also one of the modifications of the mind.

No, awareness is not part of the mind. It flows through the mind, but it is not part of the mind. It is just like this bulb: the electricity flows through it, but the electricity is not part of the bulb. If you break the bulb you have not broken the electricity. The expression will be hindered, but the potentiality remains hidden. You put in another bulb and the electricity starts flowing.

Mind is just an instrument. Awareness is not part of it, but awareness flows through it. When mind is transcended, awareness remains in itself. That's why I say even a Buddha will have to use the mind if he talks to you, if he relates to you, because then he will need flow, flow of his inner pool. He will have to use instruments, mediums, and then mind will function. But mind is just a vehicle.

You move in a vehicle, but you are not the vehicle. You go in a car or you fly in an aircraft, but you are not the vehicle. Mind is just the vehicle. And you are not using the mind to its total capacity. If you use it to its total capacity, it will become right-knowledge.

We are using our mind as if someone can use an airplane as a bus. You can cut the wings off the airplane and use it like a bus on the road. That will do, it will work like a bus—but you are foolish. That bus can fly! You are not using it to its right capacity.

You are using your mind for dreams, imaginations, madness. You have not used it, you have cut the wings. If you use it with the wings it can become right-knowledge, it can become wisdom. But that too is part of the mind, that too is the vehicle. The user remains behind; the user cannot be the used. You are using it, you are awareness. And all the efforts for meditation mean to know this awareness in its purity, without any medium. Once you know it without any instrument.... You can know it. And this can be known only when mind has stopped functioning. When mind has stopped functioning you will become aware that awareness is there, you are filled with it. Mind was just a vehicle, a passage. Now if you want you can use the mind, if you don't want you need not use it.

Body, mind, both are vehicles. You are not the vehicle, you are the master hidden behind these vehicles. But you have forgotten completely. And you have become the cart, you have become the vehicle. This is what Gurdjieff calls identification. This is what in India yogis have called tadatmya, becoming one with something which you are not.

The fifth question:
Please explain how it is possible that just by looking, by witnessing the recordings in the brain cells, the sources of thought-process can cease to be.

They never cease to be, but just by witnessing identification is broken. Buddha lived in his body for forty years after his enlightenment, the body did not cease. Continuously, for forty years he was talking, explaining, making people understand what had happened to him and how the same can happen to them. He was using the mind, the mind had not ceased. And when he came back to his home town after twelve years he recognized his father, he recognized his wife, he recognized his son. The mind was there, the memory was there; otherwise recognition is impossible. The mind had not really ceased.

When we say the mind ceases, we mean your identification is broken. Now you know this is the mind and this is 'I am'. The bridge is broken. Now the mind is not the master. It has become just an instrument, it has fallen to its right place. So whenever you need it you can use it. It is just like a fan: if you want to use it we put it on, then the fan starts functioning. Right now we are not using the fan so it is non-functioning. But it is there, it has not ceased to be. Any moment you can use it. It has not disappeared.

Just by witnessing identification disappears, not the mind. But by identification disappearing, you are a totally new being. For the first time you have come to know your real phenomenon, your real reality. For the first time you have come to know who you are. Now mind is just part of the mechanism around you.

It is just as if you are a pilot and flying an airplane: you use many instruments, your eyes are working on many instruments continuously aware of this and that, but you are not the instruments.

This mind, this body and many functions of the body-mind, are just around you—the mechanism. In this mechanism you can exist in two ways. One way of existence is forgetting yourself and feeling as if you are the mechanism. This is bondage, this is misery; this is the world, the sansar.

Another way of functioning is this: becoming alert that you are separate, you are different. Then you go on using, but now it makes a lot of difference—now the mechanism is not you. And if something goes wrong in the mechanism you can try to put it right, but you will not be disturbed. Even if the whole mechanism disappears you will not be disturbed.

Buddha dying and you dying are two different phenomena. Buddha knows only the mechanism is dying. It has been used and now there is no need. A burden has been removed, he is becoming free. Now he will move without form. But you dying is totally different: you are suffering, you are crying because you feel you are dying, not the mechanism. It is your death; then it becomes an intense suffering.

Just by witnessing, mind doesn't cease and the brain cells will not cease. Rather, they will become more alive because there will be less conflict, more energy. They will become more fresh. And you can use them more rightly, more accurately, but you will not be burdened by them and they will not force you to do something. They will not push and pull you here and there. You will be the master.

But how does it happen just by witnessing? Because it has happened, the bondage has happened, by not witnessing. The bondage has happened because you are not alert, so the bondage will disappear if you become alert. The bondage is only unawareness. Nothing else is needed but becoming more alert, whatsoever you do.

You are sitting here listening to me. You can listen with awareness, you can listen without awareness. Without awareness listening will also be there, but it will be a different thing, the quality will differ. Then your ears are listening and your mind is functioning somewhere else.

Then, somehow, a few words will penetrate you and they will be mixed, and your mind will interpret them in its own way. It will put its own ideas into them. Everything will be a muddle and a mess. You have listened but many things will be bypassed, you will not listen to many things, you will choose. Then the whole thing will be distorted.

If you are alert, the moment you become alert thinking ceases. With alertness you cannot think. The whole energy becomes alert, there is no energy left to move into thinking. When you are alert even for a single moment, you simply listen. There is no barrier. Your words are not there which can get mixed. You need not interpret. The impact is direct.

If you can listen with alertness, then what I am saying may be meaningful or may not be meaningful, but your listening with alertness will always be significant in meaning. That very alertness will make a peak of your consciousness. The past will dissolve, the future will disappear. You will be nowhere else, you will be just here and now.

And in that moment of silence when thinking is not, you will be deep in contact with your own source. And that source is bliss, and that source is divine. So the only thing to be done is to do everything with alertness.

The last question:

While talking on Lao Tzu you become a Taoist sage, while talking on Tantra you become a tantrika, while talking on bhakti you become an enlightened bhakta, and while talking on Yoga you have become a perfect yogi. Will you please explain how this phenomenon has become possible?

If you are not, only then it can become possible. If you are, then it cannot become possible. If you are not, if the host has completely disappeared, then the guest becomes the host. So the guest may be Lao Tzu, the guest may be Patanjali. The host is not there, so the guest takes the place completely, he becomes the host. If you are not, then you can become.Patanjali; there is no difficulty. You can become Krishna, you can become Christ. If you are there, then it is very difficult. And if you are there, whatsoever you say will be wrong.

That's why I say these are not commentaries. I am not commenting on Patanjali. I am simply absent, allowing Patanjali. So it is not a commentary.

'Commentary' means that, "Patanjali is something separate, and I am something separate, and I am commenting on Patanjali"—it is bound to be distorted because how can you comment on Patanjali? Whatsoever I say would be my saying, and whatsoever I say would be my interpretation. It cannot be of Patanjali himself. And that's not good. That is destructive. So I am not commenting at all. I am simply allowing, and this allowing is possible if you are not:

If you become a witness, the ego disappears. And when the ego disappears you become a vehicle, you become a passage, you become a flute. And the flute can be put on Patanjali's lips, and the flute can be put on Krishna's lips, and the flute can be put on Buddha's lips—the flute remains the same. But when it is on Buddha's lips, Buddha is flowing.

So this is not a commentary. This is difficult to understand because you cannot allow. You are so much inside you cannot allow anyone. And these are not persons. Patanjali is not a person: Patanjali is a presence. If you are absent, his presence can function.

And if you ask Patanjali, he will say the same. If you ask Patanjali, he will not say that these sutras have been created by him. He will say, "These are very ancient—sanatan." He will say, "Millions and millions of seers have seen them. I am just a vehicle.

I am absent and they are speaking." If you ask Krishna, he will say, "I am not speaking. This is the ancientmost message. It has been always so." And if you ask Jesus, he will say, "I am no more, I am not there."

Why this insistence? Anybody who becomes absent, who becomes a non-ego, starts functioning as a vehicle, as a passage—a passage for all that is true, a passage for all that is hidden in existence, that can flow. And you will be able to understand whatsoever I am saying only when even for moments you will be absent.

If you are too much there, your ego is there, then whatsoever I am saying cannot flow in you. It is not only an intellectual communication. It is something deeper.

If you are a non-ego even for a single moment, then the impact will be felt. Then something unknown has entered in you, and in that moment you will understand. And there is no other way to understand.

Enough for today?

5

RIGHT KNOWLEDGE

7. प्रत्यक्षानुमानागमाः प्रमाणानि ।

*Right-knowledge has three sources:
direct cognition, inference and the
words of the awakened ones.*

8. विपर्ययोमिथ्याज्ञानमतद्रूप प्रतिष्ठम् ।

*Wrong-knowledge is a false
conception not corresponding to the
thing as it is.*

9. शब्दज्ञानानुपाती वस्तुशून्यो विकल्पः ।

*An image conjured up by words
without any substance behind it is
vikalpa, imagination.*

10. अभाव प्रत्ययालम्बन वृत्तिर्निद्रा ।

*The modification of the mind which is
based on the absence of any content
in it, is sleep.*

11. अनुभूतविषयासम्प्रमोषः स्मृतिः ।

*Memory is the calling up of past
experiences.*

The first sutra:
Right-knowledge has three sources:
direct cognition, inference and the
words of the awakened ones.

Pratyaksha, direct cognition, is the first source of right-knowledge. Direct cognition means a face-to-face encounter without any mediator, without any medium, without any agent. When you know something directly, the knower faces the known immediately. There is no one to relate, no bridge. Then it is right-knowledge. But then many problems arise.

Ordinarily, pratyaksha, direct cognition, has been translated, interpreted, commented on, in a very wrong way. The very word 'pratyaksha' means before the eyes, in front of the eyes. But eyes themselves are a mediation, the knower is hidden behind. Eyes are the medium. You are hearing me but this is not direct, this is not immediate. You are hearing me through the senses, through the ears. You are seeing me through the eyes.

Your eyes can wrongly report to you, your ears can wrongly report. No one should be believed; no mediator should be

135

believed because you cannot rely on the mediator. If your eyes are ill they will report differently, if your eyes are drugged they will report differently, if your eyes are filled with memory they will report differently.

If you are in love then you see something else; if you are not in love then you can never see that. An ordinary woman can become the most beautiful person in the world if you see through love. When your eyes are filled with love then they report something else. And the same person can appear the ugliest if your eyes are filled with hate. They are not reliable.

You hear through the ears. Ears are just instruments, they can function wrongly; they can hear something which has not been said, they can miss something which was being said. Senses cannot be reliable, senses are just mechanical devices.

Then what is pratyaksha, then what is direct cognition? Direct cognition can only be when there is no mediator, not even the senses. Patanjali says then it is right-knowledge. This is the first basic source of right-knowledge: when you know something and you need not depend on anybody else.

You transcend the senses only in deep meditation. Then direct cognition becomes possible. When Buddha comes to know his innermost being, that innermost being is pratyaksha, that is direct cognition. No senses are involved, nobody has reported it, there is no one like an agent. The knower and known are face to face, there is nothing in between. This is immediacy, and only immediacy can be true.

So the first right-knowledge can only be that of the inner self. You may know the whole world, but if you have not known the innermost core of your being your whole knowledge is absurd, it is not really knowledge; it cannot be true because the first, basic, right-knowledge has not happened to you. Your whole edifice is false. You may know many things… if you have not known yourself all your knowledge is based on reports, reports given by the senses. But how can you be certain that the senses are reporting rightly?

In the night you dream. While dreaming you start believing in the dream, that it is true. Your senses are reporting the dream— your eyes are seeing it, your ears are hearing it, you may be touching it. Your senses are reporting to you, that's why you fall under the illusion that it is real. You are here… it may be just a dream. How can you be certain that I am speaking to you, in reality? It is possible it may be just a dream—you are dreaming me. Every dream is true while you dream.

Chuang Tzu once saw in a dream that he had become a butterfly. And in the morning he was sad. His disciples asked, "Why are you so sad?"

Chuang Tzu said, "I am in trouble. I have never been in such trouble before. This puzzle seems to be impossible, it cannot be solved. Last night I saw in a dream that I have become a butterfly."

The disciples laughed. They said, "What is there? This is not a riddle. A dream is just a dream."

Chuang Tzu said, "But listen, I am troubled. If Chuang Tzu can dream that he has become a butterfly, a butterfly may be dreaming now that she has become Chuang Tzu. So how to decide whether I am now facing reality or again a dream? And if Chuang Tzu can become a butterfly why can't a butterfly dream that she has become a Chuang Tzu?"

There is no impossibility, the reverse can occur. You cannot rely on the senses. In dreams they deceive you. If you take a drug, lsd or something, your senses will start deceiving you; you will start seeing things which are not there. They can deceive you to such an extent that you can start believing things so absolutely that you will be in danger.

One girl in New York jumped from the sixtieth floor because under lsd she now thought she could fly. Chuang Tzu was not wrong: the girl really flew out of the window. Of course, she died. But she will never be able to know that she had been deceived by her senses under the influence of the drug.

Even without drugs we have illusions. You are passing through a dark street and suddenly you get scared... there is a snake. You start running, and later on you come to know that there was no snake, just a rope was lying there. But when you felt that there was a snake, there was a snake. Your eyes were reporting that the snake was there and you behaved accordingly—you escaped from the place.

Senses cannot be believed. Then what is direct cognition? Direct cognition is something which is known without the senses. So the first right-knowledge can only be of the inner self, because only there will the senses not be needed. Everywhere else the senses will be needed. If you want to see me you will have to see through the eyes, but if you want to see yourself eyes are not needed. Even a blind man can see himself. If you want to see me light will be needed, but if you want to see yourself darkness is okay, light is not needed.

Even in the darkest cave you can know yourself. No medium—light, eyes, anything—is needed. The inner experience is immediate, and that immediate experience is the basis of all right-knowledge.

Once you are rooted in that inner experience then many

things will start happening to you. It will not be possible to understand them right now. One who is rooted in his center, in his inner being, one who has come upon it, to feel it as a direct experience, then the senses cannot deceive him. He is awakened. Then his eyes cannot deceive him, then his ears cannot deceive him, then nothing can deceive him. Deception has dropped.

You can be deceived because you are living in delusion. You cannot be deceived once you have come to be a right knower. You cannot be deceived! Then everything, by and by, takes the shape of right-knowledge. Once you know yourself, then whatsoever you know will automatically fall into being right because now you are right. This is the distinction to be remembered: if you are right then everything becomes right, if you are wrong then everything goes wrong. So it is not a question of doing something outside, it is a question of doing something inside.

You cannot deceive a buddha—it is impossible. How can you deceive a buddha? He is rooted in himself. You are transparent to him, you cannot deceive him. Before you know, he knows you. Even a glimmer of thought in you is clearly seen by him. He penetrates you to your very being.

Your penetration goes to the same extent in others as it goes into yourself. If you can penetrate into yourself, you can penetrate into everything to the same extent. The deeper you move within, the deeper you can move without. And you have not moved within even a single inch, so whatsoever you do outside is just like a dream.

Patanjali says, the first source of right-knowledge is immediate, direct cognition, pratyaksha. He is not concerned with charvakas, the old materialists, who said that pratyaksha, only that which is before the eyes, is true.

Because of this word 'pratyaksha', direct cognition, much misunderstanding has happened. The Indian school of materialists is charvaka. The source of Indian materialism was Brihaspati, a very penetrating thinker, but a thinker; a very profound philosopher but a philosopher, not a realized soul. He says only pratyaksha is true, and by pratyaksha he means whatsoever you know through the senses is true. And he says there is no way of knowing anything without the senses, so only sense-knowledge is real for charvakas.

Hence he denies there can be any God because no one has ever seen him. And only that which can be seen can be real, that which cannot be seen cannot be real. God is not because you cannot see, the soul is not because you cannot see. And he says, "If there is a God, bring him before me so I can see. If I see, then he is, because only seeing is truth."

He also uses the word 'pratyaksha', direct cognition, but his meaning is totally different. When Patanjali uses the word 'pratyaksha' his meaning is on an altogether different level. He says, immediate knowledge not derived from any instrument, not derived from any medium is true. And once this knowledge happens you have become true. And now nothing false can happen to you. When you are true, authentically rooted in truth, then illusions become impossible.

That's why it is said that buddhas never dream; one who is awakened never dreams. Because even dreams cannot happen to him, he cannot be deceived. He sleeps, but not like you. He sleeps in a totally different way, the quality is different. Only his body sleeps, relaxes. His being remains alert. And that alertness won't allow any dreaming to happen.

You can dream only when alertness is lost. When you are not aware, when you are deeply hypnotized, then you start dreaming. Dreaming can happen only when you are completely unaware. The more unawareness, the more dreams will be there; the more awareness, the less dreams—fully aware, no dreams. Even dreaming becomes impossible for one who is rooted in himself, who has come to know the inner being immediately.

This is the first source of right-knowledge. The second source is inference. That is secondary, but that too is worth consideration because, as you are right now, you don't know whether there is a self within or not. You have no direct knowledge of your inner being. What to do? There are two possibilities. You can simply deny, that there is no inner core of your being, there is no soul, as charvakas do; or in the West as Epicurus, Marx, Engels and others have done.

But Patanjali says that if you know there is no need for inference, but if you don't know then too it will be helpful to infer. For example, Descartes, one of the greatest thinkers of the West, started his philosophical quest through doubt. He took the standpoint from the very beginning that he will not believe in anything which is not indubitable. That which could be doubted, he would doubt. And he would try to find out a point which could not be doubted, and only on that point would he create the whole edifice of his thinking. A beautiful quest—honest, arduous, dangerous.

So he denied God, because you can doubt it. Many have doubted and no one has been able to answer their doubts. He went on denying. Whatsoever could be doubted, conceived to be dubitable, he denied. For years he was continuously in an inner turmoil. Then he fell upon the point which was indubitable: he couldn't deny himself, that was impossible. You cannot say, "I am not." If you say it, your very saying proves that you are. So this was the basic rock—"I cannot deny myself, I cannot say I am not. Who will say it? Even to doubt, I am needed."

This is inference. This is not direct cognition. This is through logic and argument—but it gives a shadow, it gives a glimpse, it gives you a possibility, an opening. And then Descartes had the rock, and on this rock a great temple can be built. One indubitable fact and you can reach to the absolute truth. If you start with a doubtful thing you will never reach anywhere. In the very base, doubt remains.

Patanjali says, inference is the second source of right-knowledge. Right-logic, right-doubting, right-argument can give you something which can help towards real knowledge. That he calls inference, anuman. You have not seen directly, but everything proves it; it must be so. There are situational proofs that it must be so.

For example, you look around the vast universe. You may not be able to conceive that there is a God, but you cannot deny; even through simple inference you cannot deny that the whole world is a system, a coherent whole, a design. That cannot be denied. The design is so apparent, even science cannot deny it. Rather, on the contrary, science goes on finding more and more designs, more and more laws.

If the world is just an accident then science is impossible. But the world doesn't seem to be an accident, it seems to be planned. And it is running according to certain laws and those laws are never broken.

Patanjali will say that design in the universe cannot be denied, and if once you feel there is design, the designer has entered. But that is an inference, you have not known him directly—but the design of the universe, the planning, the law, the order; and the order is so superb, it is so min-ute, so superb, so infinite—the order is there. Everything is humming with an order, a musical harmony of the whole universe. Someone seems to be hidden behind, but that's an inference. Patanjali says inference can also be a help towards right-knowledge, but it has to be right-inference. Logic is dangerous, it is double-edged. You can use logic wrongly, then too you will reach conclusions.

For example, I told you that the plan is there, the design is there; the world has an order, a beautiful order, perfect. Right-inference will be that there seems to be somebody's hand behind it. We may not be directly aware, we may not be in direct touch with that hand but a hand seems to be there, hidden. This is the right-inference.

But from the same premises you can also infer wrongly. There have been thinkers who have said… Diderot has said, "Because of order I cannot believe there is a God. In the world there seems to be perfect order. Because of this order, I cannot believe in God." What is his logic? He says if there is a person behind it, then there cannot be so much order. If a person is behind it then he must commit mistakes sometimes. Sometimes he must go whimsical, crazy, sometimes he will change. Laws cannot be so perfect if someone is behind them. Laws can be perfect if there is no one behind them and they are simply mechanical.

That too has an appeal. If everything goes perfectly, it looks mechanical because man…. It is said, to err is human. If some person is there then he must err sometimes; he will get bored with so much perfection. And sometimes he must like to change.

Water boils at one hundred degrees. It has been boiling at

one hundred degrees for millennia, always and always. God must get bored. "If someone is behind," Diderot says, "so just for a change, one day he will say, 'From now onwards the water will boil at ninety degrees.'" But it has never happened, so there seems to be no person.

Both arguments look perfect. But Patanjali says, right-inference is that which gives you possibilities of growth. It is not a question whether the logic is perfect or not. The question is, your conclusion should become an opening. If there is no God it becomes a closing. Then you cannot grow. If you conclude there is some hidden hand, the world becomes a mystery. And then you are not here just by accident. Then your life becomes meaningful. Then you are part of a great scheme. Then something is possible, you can do something, you can rise in awareness.

A right-inference means one which can give you growth, that which can give you growth; a wrong-inference, howsoever perfect looking, is that which closes your growth. Inference can also be a source of right-knowledge. Even logic can be used to be a source of right-knowledge, but you have to be very aware about what you are doing. If you are just logical you may commit suicide through it. Logic can become a suicide—for many it becomes.

Just a few days before one seeker from California was here. He traveled long… he had come to meet me. And then he said, "Before I can meditate, or before you tell me to meditate—because I have heard that whosoever comes to you, you push them into meditation—so before you push me in, I have got many questions." He had a list of at least a hundred questions. I think he has not left out any that are possible… about God, about soul, about truth, about heaven and hell and everything—a sheet full of questions. He said, "Unless you solve these questions first, I am not going to meditate."

He is logical in a way because he says, "Unless my questions are answered how can I meditate? Unless I feel confident that you are right, you have answered my doubts, how can I go in some direction you show and indicate? You may be wrong. So you can prove your rightness only if my doubts disappear."

And his doubts are such that they cannot disappear. This is the dilemma: if he meditates they can disappear, but he says he will meditate only when these doubts are not there. What to do? He says, "First prove there is a God." No one has ever proved it, no one ever can. That doesn't mean that God is not there, but he cannot be proved. He is not a small thing which can be proved or disproved. It is such a vital thing that you have to live it to know it. No proof can help.

But logically he is right. He says, "Unless you prove, how can I start? If there is no soul, who is going to meditate? So first prove that there is a self, then I can meditate."

This man is committing suicide. No one will ever be able to answer him. He has created all the barriers, and through these barriers he will not be able to grow. But he is logical. What should I do with such a person? If I start answering his questions, a person who can create a hundred doubts can create millions, because doubting is a way, a style of mind. You can answer one question, through your answer he will create ten because the mind remains the same.

He looks for doubts, and if I answer logically I am helping his logical mind to be fed, to be more strengthened. I am feeding it; that will not help. He has to be brought out of his logicalness. So I asked him, "Have you ever been in love?"

He said, "But why? You are changing the subject."

I said, "I will come to your points, but suddenly it has become very meaningful to me to ask have you ever loved."

He said, "Yes!" His face changed.

I asked, "But you loved before, or before falling in love, you doubted the whole phenomenon?"

Then he was disturbed. He was uncomfortable. He said, "No, I never thought about it. I had simply fallen in love, and then only I became aware."

So I said, "You do the opposite: first think about love, whether love is possible, whether love exists, whether love can exist. And first let it be proved. And make it a condition that unless it is proved you will not love anybody."

He said, "What are you saying? You will destroy my life. If I make this a condition, then I cannot love."

"But," I told him, "this is the same that you are doing. Meditation is just like love, you have to know it first. God is just like love. That's why Jesus goes on saying that God is love. It is just like love. First one has to experience."

A logical mind can be closed, and so logically that he will never feel that he has closed his own doors to all the possibilities for all growth. So inference, anuman, means thinking in such a way that growth is helped. Then it can become a source of right-knowledge.

And the third is most beautiful, and nowhere else has it been made a source of right-knowledge: the words of the awakened ones, agama. There has been a long controversy about this third source. Patanjali says you can know directly, then it is okay. You can infer rightly, then too you are on the right path and you will reach the source.

But there are a few things you cannot even infer, and you have not known. But you are not the first on this Earth, you are not the first seeker. Millions have been seeking for millions of ages, and not only on this planet but on other planets also. The search is eternal, and many have arrived. They have reached the goal, they have entered the temple. Their words are also a source of right-knowledge.

Agama means the words of those who have known. Buddha says something or Jesus says something: we don't know what he is saying, we have not experienced that, so we have no way of judging it. We don't know what and how to infer rightly through his words. And the words are contradictory so you can infer anything you like.

There are a few who think Jesus was neurotic. Western psychiatrists have been trying to prove that he was neurotic, he was a maniac. These claims that, "I am the son of God, and the only son"—he was mad, an egomaniac, neurotic. It can be proved that he was neurotic because there are many neurotic people who claim such things. You can find out; in madhouses there are many people....

It happened once in Baghdad. Caliph Omar was the king, and one man declared on the streets of Baghdad, "I am the paigambara, I am the messenger, I am the prophet. And now Mohammed is cancelled because I am here. I am the last word, the last message from the divine. And now there is no need for Mohammed, he is just out of date. He was the messenger up to now but now I have come. Now you can forget Mohammed."

It was not a Hindu country. Hindus can tolerate everything; no one has tolerated like the Hindus. They can tolerate everything because they say, "Unless we know exactly we cannot say yes, we cannot say no. He may be the messenger, who knows?"

But Mohammedans are different—very dogmatic. They cannot tolerate. So Caliph Omar, having caught the new prophet, threw him in jail and told him, "Twenty-four hours are being given to you. Reconsider. And if you say you are not the prophet, that Mohammed is the prophet, then you will be released. If you insist in your madness, then after twenty-four hours I will come to the jail and you will be killed."

The man laughed. He said, "Look! This is written in the scripture—that prophets will always be treated like this, as you are treating me." He was logical. Mohammed himself was treated like that, so this was nothing new. The man said to Omar, "This is nothing new. This is how things are naturally going to be. And I am not in any position to reconsider. I am not the authority, I am just the messenger. Only God can change. In twenty-four hours you can come, you will find me the same. Only he can change who has appointed me."

While this talk was going on another madman, who was chained to a pillar, started laughing. So Omar asked, "Why are you laughing?"

He said, "This man is absolutely wrong. I never appointed him! I cannot allow this. After Mohammed I have not sent any messenger."

In every madhouse these people are there, and it can be proved that Jesus is a similar case.

And the words are so contradictory and illogical. And every person who has known is compelled to speak contradictorily, paradoxically, because the truth is such that it can be expressed only through paradoxes. Their statements are not clear, they are mysterious. And you can conclude anything out of them if you infer. You infer, your mind is there. The inference is going to be your inference. So Patanjali says there is a third source.

You don't know. If you know directly, then there is no question, then there is no need for any other source. If you have direct cognition, then there is no need for inference or for the words of the enlightened ones; you yourself have become enlightened. Then you can drop the other two sources. Then inference, but the inference will be yours. If you are mad then your inference will be mad. But if this has not happened, then the third source is worth trying—the words of the enlightened ones.

You cannot prove them, you cannot disprove them. You can only have a trust, and that trust is hypothetical; it is very scientific. In science also you cannot proceed without a hypothesis. But a hypothesis is not belief; it is just a working arrangement. A hypothesis is just a direction, you will have to experiment. And if the experiment proves right then the hypothesis becomes a theory. If the experiment goes wrong then the hypothesis is discarded. The words of the enlightened ones are to be taken on trust, as a hypothesis. Then work them out in your life. If they prove true, then the hypothesis has become a faith, if they prove false then the hypothesis has to be discarded.

You go to Buddha. He will say, "Wait! Be patient, meditate, and for two years don't ask any question." This you have to take on trust, there is no other way.

You can think, "This man may be just deceiving me. Then two years of my life are wasted. If after two years it is proved that this man was just hocus-pocus, just a deceiver or self-deceived, in an illusion that he has become enlightened, then my two years are wasted." But there is no other way. You have to take the risk. And if you remain there without trusting Buddha, these two years will be useless because unless you trust you cannot work. And the work is so intense that only if you have trust then you can move wholly into it, totally into it. If you don't have trust then you go on withholding something, and that withholding will not allow you to experience what Buddha is indicating

There is risk, but life itself is risk. For a higher life there will be higher risks. You move on a dangerous path. But remember, there is only one error in life, and that is not moving at all; that is, just afraid, sitting; just afraid that if you move something may go wrong, so it is better to wait and sit. This is the only error. You will not be in danger but no growth will be possible.

Patanjali says there are things which you do not know, there are things which your logic cannot infer; you have to take on trust. Because of this third source, the guru, the master, becomes a necessity—someone who knows. And you have to take the risk, and I say it is a risk because there is no guarantee. The whole thing may prove just a wastage, but it is better to take the risk because even if it is proved to be a wastage, you have learned much. Now no other person will be able to deceive you so easily. At least you have learned this much.

And if you move with trust, if you move totally, follow a Buddha like a shadow, things may start happening because they have happened to the person. They have happened to this Gautam Buddha, to Jesus, to Mahavira, and they know the path they have traveled. If you argue with them you will be the loser. They cannot be the losers, they will simply leave you aside.

In this century this has happened with Gurdjieff. So many people were attracted to him, but he would create such a situation for the new disciples that unless they could trust totally they would have to leave immediately—unless they could trust even in absurdities. And those absurdities were planned. Gurdjieff would go on lying. In the morning he would say something, in the afternoon something else. And you were not to ask! He would shatter your logical mind completely.

In the morning he would say, "Dig this ditch. And this is a must! By the evening this must be complete." And the whole day you have been digging it. You have exerted, you are tired, you are perspiring, you have not taken food, and by evening he would come and say, "Throw the mud back in the ditch. And before you go to bed it has to be completed."

Now even an ordinary mind will say, "What do you mean? I have wasted the whole day. And I was thinking it was something very necessary, by the evening it has to be completed and now you say, 'Throw the mud back!'"

If you asked such a thing Gurdjieff would say, "You simply leave! You go! I am not for you, you are not for me."

The ditch or the digging was not the thing. What he was trying was whether you could trust him even when he was absurd. And once he knew that you could trust him and you could move with him wherever he led, only then real things would follow. Then the test was over, you have been examined and found to be authentic—a real seeker who can work and who can trust. And then real things could happen to you, never before.

Patanjali is a master, and he knows this third source very well through his own experience with thousands and thousands of disciples. He must have worked with many, many disciples and seekers; only then is it possible to write such a treatise as the Yoga Sutras. They are not by a thinker, they are by one who has experimented with many types of minds and who has penetrated with many, many layers of minds, every type of person who has worked. He makes this the third source: the words of the awakened ones.

The second sutra:
Wrong-knowledge is a false conception not corresponding to the thing as it is.

Now some definitions which will be helpful later on. The definition of viparyaya, wrong-knowledge. Wrong-knowledge is a false conception of something not corresponding to the thing as it is. We all have a big burden of wrong-knowledge, because before we encounter a fact we are already prejudiced.

If you are a Hindu and someone is introduced to you and it is said that he is a Mohammedan, immediately you have taken a wrong attitude that this man must be wrong. If you are a Christian and someone is introduced as a Jew you are not going to 'dig' this man, you are not going to enter this particular man. Just by saying "a Jew" your prejudice has come in; you have already known this man. Now there is no need, you know what type of man this is—a Jew.

You have a preconception, a prejudiced mind, and this prejudiced mind gives you wrong-knowledge. All Jews are not bad; neither are all Christians good nor are all Mohammedans bad; neither are all Hindus good. Really, goodness and badness don't belong to any race, they belong to persons, individuals. There may be bad Mohammedans, bad Hindus, good Mohammedans, good Hindus. Goodness and badness do not belong to any nation, to any race, to any culture, they belong to individuals, personalities. But that's difficult, to face a person without any prejudice. And you will have a revelation.

Once it happened to me. I was traveling. I entered my compartment. And many people had come to see me off, so the person who was in the compartment, another passenger, immediately touched my feet and he said, "You must be a great saint. So many persons have come to see you off."

So I told this man, "I am a Mohammedan. I may be a great saint but I am a Mohammedan."

He felt shocked! He had touched a Mohammedan's feet and he was a brahmin! He started perspiring, he was nervous. He looked again and he said, "No, you are joking." Just to console himself he said, "You are joking."

"I am not joking. Why should I joke? You should have inquired before you touched my feet!"

Then we were both together in the compartment. Again and again he would look at me and would take a long, deep breath. He must have been thinking to go and take a bath! But he was not encountering me. I was there, and he was concerned with a concept of 'Mohammedan'. And he was a brahmin—he had become impure by touching me.

Nobody encounters things, persons, as they are—you have a prejudice. These prejudices create viparyaya, these prejudices create wrong-knowledge. Whatsoever you think, if you have not come freshly upon the fact, it is going to be wrong. Don't bring your past, don't bring your prejudices. Put aside your mind and encounter the fact. Just see whatsoever there is to be seen. Don't project.

We go on projecting. Our mind is just completely filled and fixed from the very childhood. Everything has been given to us readymade, and through that readymade knowledge our whole life becomes an illusion. You never meet a real person, you never see a real flower. Just by hearing "This is a rose" you say "Beautiful!" mechanically. You have not felt the beauty, you have not sensed the beauty, you have not touched this flower. Just "rose is beautiful" is in your mind; the moment you hear 'rose' the mind projects and says "It is beautiful."

And you may believe that you have come to feel that the rose is beautiful; this is not so. This is false. Just look. That's why children come to things more deeply than grown-up people, because they don't know names. They are not yet prejudiced. If a rose is beautiful only then will it be beautiful; all roses are not beautiful. Children come near to things, their eyes are fresh. They see things as they are because they don't know how to project anything.

But we are always in a hurry to make them grown-ups, to make them adults. We are filling their minds with knowledge, information. This is one of the most recent discoveries of psychologists: that when children enter into school they have more intelligence than when they leave the university. The latest findings prove this. When children enter in the first grade, they have more intelligence. They will have less and less intelligence as they grow in knowledge. And by the time they become bachelors and masters and doctors, they are finished. When they come back with a doctor's degree, a Ph.D., they have left their intelligence somewhere in the university. They are dead, filled with knowledge, crammed with knowledge—but this knowledge is just false, a prejudice about everything. Now they cannot feel things directly, they cannot feel live persons directly, they cannot live directly. Everything has become verbal, wordy. It is not real now, it has become mental.

Wrong-knowledge is a false conception not corresponding to

the thing as it is.

Put aside your prejudices, knowledge, conceptions, pre-formulated information and look fresh, become a child again. And this has to be done moment to moment because every moment you are gathering.

One of the oldest Yoga aphorisms is: Die every moment so you can be reborn every moment. Die every moment to the past, throw all the dust that you have collected and look afresh. But this has to be done continuously because next moment the dust has gathered again.

Nan-in was in search of a Zen master when he was a seeker. He lived with his master for many years, and then the master said, "Everything is okay. You have almost achieved."

But he said 'almost', so Nan-in said, "What do you mean?"

The master said, "I will have to send you to another master for a few days. That will do the last finishing touch." Nan-in was very much excited. He said, "Send me immediately!" A letter was given to him. And he was so excited, he thought he was being sent to someone who was a greater master than his own. But when he reached to the man he was no one—just a keeper of an inn, a doorkeeper of an inn.

He felt very much disappointed and he thought, "This must be some sort of joke. This man is going to be my last master? He is going to give me the finishing touch?" But he had come, so he thought, "It is better to be here for a few days at least to rest, then I will go back. It was a long journey." So he said to the innkeeper, "My master has given this letter."

The innkeeper said, "But I cannot read, so you can keep your letter; it is not needed. And you can be here."

Nan-in said, "But I have been sent to learn something from you."

The innkeeper said, "I am just an innkeeper. I am not a master, I am not a teacher. There must have been some misunderstanding. You may have come to a wrong person. I am just an innkeeper. I cannot teach, I don't know anything. But since you have come you can just watch me. That may be helpful. You rest and watch."

But there was nothing to watch. In the morning he would open the door of the inn. Then guests would come and he would clean their things—the pots, the utensils and everything—and he would serve. And in the night again, when everybody had gone and the guests had gone to sleep to their beds, he would clean things again, pots, utensils, everything. And in the morning, again the same.

By the third day Nan-in was bored. And he said, "There is nothing to watch. You go on cleaning utensils, you go on doing ordinary work, so I must leave." The innkeeper laughed, but said nothing.

Nan-in went back. He was very angry with his master and said, "Why? Why was I sent for such a long journey? It was tedious, and the man was just an innkeeper. And he didn't teach me anything, and he simply said, 'Watch'—and there was nothing to watch."

But the master said, "Still, you were there for three, four days. Even if there was nothing to watch, you must have watched. What were you doing?"

So he said, "I was watching! In the night he would clean the utensils, pots, put everything there, and in the morning he was again cleaning."

The master said, "This! This is the teaching! This is for what you were sent! He had cleaned those pots in the night, but in the morning he was again cleaning those clean pots. What does it mean? Because even in the night, when nothing had happened, they had become unclean again, some dust had settled again. So you may be pure—now you are—you may be innocent, but every moment you have to continue cleaning. You may not do anything, still you become impure just by the passage of time. Moment to moment, just the passage... not doing anything, just sitting under a tree, you become unclean. And that uncleanliness is not because you were doing something bad or something wrong, it happens just through the passage of time. Dust collects, so you go on cleaning. And this is the last touch. Because I feel you have become proud that you are pure and now you are not aware of a constant effort to clean."

Moment to moment one has to die and be reborn again. Only then are you freed from wrong-knowledge.

The third sutra:
An image conjured up by words without any substance behind it is vikalpa, imagination.

Imagination is just through words, verbal structures. You create a thing—it is not there, it is not a reality, but you create it through your mental images. And you can create it to such an extent that you yourself become deceived by it and you think it is real. This happens in hypnosis. Hypnotize a person and say anything; he conjures up the image and that image becomes real. You can do it. You are doing it in many ways.

One of the most famous Swedish actresses, Greta Garbo, has written a memoir. She was an ordinary girl, just a homely, ordinary girl, very poor, and working in a barber shop. Just for few pennies she would put soap on the customers' faces. For three years she was doing that.

One day, one American film director was there in that barber shop and she was putting soap on his face, and just the way Americans are—he may not have even meant it—he simply looked in the mirror, the reflection of the girl, and said, "How beautiful!" And Greta Garbo was born that very moment.

She writes that suddenly she became different. She had never thought herself beautiful, she couldn't conceive of it. And she had never heard anybody saying that she was beautiful. For the first time she also looked in the mirror and the face was different—this man had made her beautiful. And her whole life changed. She followed the man and became one of the most famous film actresses.

What happened? Just a hypnosis, a hypnosis through a word 'beautiful', worked. It works, it becomes chemical. Everybody believes something about himself: that belief becomes reality because that belief starts working on you.

Imagination is a force, but it is a conjured-up force, an imagined force. You can use it and you can be used by it. If you can use it, it will be helpful, but if you are used by it, it is fatal, it is dangerous. Imagination can become madness any moment. Imagination can be helpful if through it you create a situation for your inner growth and crystallization. But it is through words, a conjured-up thing.

For human beings words, language, verbal constructions have become so significant that now nothing is more significant. If someone suddenly says, "Fire!" the word 'fire' will change you immediately. There may be no fire…. You will stop listening to me. There will be no effort to stop; suddenly you will stop listening to me, you will start running here and there. The word 'fire' has taken your imagination.

And you are influenced by words that way. The people in the advertisement business know what words to use to conjure up images. Through those words they catch you, they catch the whole market. There are many such words. They go on changing with the fashions.

For these few years 'new' is the word. So everything, if you look in the advertisements, is new—a 'new' Lux soap. Lux soap won't do, the new appeals immediately. Everybody is for the new. Everybody is searching for the new, something new, because everybody is bored with the old. So anything new has appeal. That may not be better than the old—it may be worse—but just the word 'new' opens vistas in the mind.

These words and their influence have to be understood deeply. For a person who is in search of the truth he must be aware of the influence of words. Politicians, advertising people—they are using words and they can create through words, such imagination that you can even stake your life; you can throw your life away just for words.

What are these?—'nation', 'the national flag'—just words. 'Hinduism'...you can say "Hinduism is in danger" and suddenly many people are ready to do something or even to die—just a few words! "Our nation is insulted": what is 'our nation'?—just words. A flag is nothing but a piece of cloth, but a whole nation can die for the flag because someone has insulted the flag, lowered it. What nonsense goes on in this world because of words. Words are dangerous, they have deep sources of influence within you. They trigger something in you and you can be captured.

Patanjali says, imagination has to be understood, because on the path of meditation words will have to be dropped so that influence by others can be dropped. Remember, words are taught by others, you are not born with words. They are taught to you and through words, many prejudices. Through words religion, through words myths—everything is fed. The word is the medium, the vehicle of culture, society, information.

You cannot excite animals to fight for a nation. You cannot excite them because they don't know what a 'nation' is. That's why there are no wars. In the animal kingdom there are no wars, no flags, no temples, no mosques. And if animals can look at us, they are bound to think that man has some obsession with words, because wars go on around them, millions are killed just because of words.

Someone is a Jew, kill him—just the word 'Jew'. Change the label, he becomes a Christian, and then there is no need to kill. But he is not ready to change the label. He will say, "I would rather be killed but I cannot change my label. I am a Jew." He is also adamant, others are also adamant. But just words!

Jean-Paul Sartre has written his autobiography and he has given it the title Words. It is beautiful, because as far as mind is concerned the whole autobiography of any mind consists of words and nothing else. And Patanjali says one has to be aware of this, because on the path of meditation words have to be left behind. Nations, religions, scriptures, languages, they have to be left behind and man has to become innocent, freed of words. When you are free of words there will be no imagination, and when there is no imagination you can face truth. Otherwise you will go on creating.

If you go to meet God, you must meet him without any words. If you have some words, he may not fit and suit your idea.

Because if a Hindu thinks he has one thousand hands and if God comes with only two hands, he will reject: "You are not a God at all. With only two hands? God has a thousand hands. Show me your other hands, only then can I believe."

It happened: one of the most beautiful persons of this past century was Sai Baba of Shirdi. He had a friend and a follower. Sai Baba was a Mohammedan. Or, no one knows whether he was a Mohammedan or a Hindu, but he lived in a mosque so it was believed that he was a Mohammedan. And a Hindu follower was there who loved, respected, had much faith in Sai Baba. Every day he would come for his darshan, and unless he saw him he would not go. Sometimes it would happen that for the whole day he would have to wait, but without seeing he would not go, and he would not take food unless he had seen Sai Baba.

Once it happened that the whole day passed, there was a big gathering and much crowding; he couldn't enter. When everybody had gone, just in the night he touched his feet.

Sai Baba said to him, "Why do you wait unnecessarily? There is no need to see me here, I can come there. And drop this; from tomorrow, now I will come. You will see me every day before you take your food."

The disciple was very happy. So next day he was waiting and waiting: nothing happened. Many things happened really—but nothing happened according to his conception. By the evening he was very angry. He had not taken food and Sai Baba had not appeared, so he went again. He said, "You promise and you don't fulfill?"

Sai Baba said, "But I appeared thrice, not even once. First time I came I was a beggar, and you said to me, 'Move away.

Don't come here.' The second time I came I was an old woman, and you just wouldn't look at me; you closed your eyes"— because the disciple had the habit of not seeing women; he was practicing not seeing women, so he closed his eyes. Sai Baba said, "I had come, but what do you expect? Should I enter your closed eyes? I was standing there but you closed your eyes. The moment you saw me you closed the eyes. Then the third time I came as a dog, and you wouldn't allow me in. You were standing at the door with a stick."

And these three things had happened. And these things have been happening to the whole humanity. The divine comes in many forms but you have a prejudice; you have a pre-formulated conception, you cannot see. He must appear according to you—and he never appears according to you, and he will never appear according to you. You cannot be the rule for him and you cannot put any conditions.

When all imagination falls away, only then truth appears. Otherwise imagination goes on making conditions and truth cannot appear. Only in a naked mind, in a nude, empty mind, truth appears, because you cannot distort it.

The fourth sutra:
The modification of the mind which is based on the absence of any content in it is sleep.

This is the definition of sleep, the fourth modification of the mind: when there is no content. Mind is always with content, except in sleep. Something or other is there. Some thought is moving, some passion is moving, some desire is moving, some memory, some future imagination, some word, something is

162

moving. Something continues continuously. Only when you are fast asleep, deeply asleep, contents stop. Mind disappears and you are in yourself without any content.

This has to be remembered because this is going to be the state of samadhi also, with only one difference: you will be aware. In sleep you are unaware, mind goes completely to non-existence. You are alone, left alone—no thought, just your being. But you are not aware. Mind is not there to disturb you, but you are not aware. Otherwise sleep can become enlightenment.

Contentless consciousness is there, but the consciousness is not alert. It is hidden, just in a seed. In samadhi the seed is broken, the consciousness becomes alert. And when consciousness is alert and there is no content, this is the goal. Sleep with awareness is the goal.

This is the fourth modification of the mind—sleep. But that goal, sleep with awareness, is not a modification of the mind, it is beyond mind. Awareness is beyond mind. If you can join sleep and awareness together, you have become enlightened. But it is difficult because even when we are awake in the day we are not alert. Even when we are awake we are not awake; the word is false. When we sleep how can we be awake?—when we are awake we are not awake.

So one has to start in the day, when you are awake. You have to be more awake, more and more intensely awake. And then you have to try with dreams: in dreams you have to be alert. Only if you succeed with the waking state; then with the dreaming state, then you will be able to succeed with the third state, of sleep.

Try first walking on the street: try to be aware. Don't just go on walking automatically, mechanically. Be alert of every movement, of every breath that you take—exhale, inhale—be alert. Of every eye movement you are doing, of every person you look at, be alert. Whatever you are doing, be alert and do it with alertness.

And then in the night, while you are falling asleep, try to remain alert. The last phase of the day will be passing, memories will be floating—remain alert and try to fall asleep with alertness. It will be difficult, but if you try, within a few weeks you will have a glimpse: you are asleep and alert. Even for a single moment... and it is so beautiful, it is so bliss-filled that you will never be the same again.

And then you will not say that sleep is just wasting time. It can become the most precious sadhana, because when the waking state goes and the sleeping starts there is a change, a change of gears inside. It is just like a change of gears in a car. When you change gears from one gear to another, for a single moment between these two there is a neutral gear, there is no gear. That moment of neutrality is very significant.

The same happens in the mind. When from waking you move into sleep, there is a moment when you are neither awake nor asleep. In that moment there is no gear, the mechanism is not functioning. Your automatic personality is nullified in that moment. In that moment your old habits will not force you in a certain pattern. In that moment you can escape and become alert.

In India this moment has been called sandhya, the moment in between. There are two sandhyas, two in-between moments: one in the night when you go from waking to sleep, and the other in the morning when you again move from sleep to waking. And these two Hindus have called the moments of prayer, sandhyakal, the period in between, because then for a single moment your personality is not there. In that single moment you are pure, innocent. If in that moment you can become alert, your whole life will have changed. You have put a base for transformation.

And then try to be alert in the dream state. There are methods for how to be alert in a dream state. Do one thing, if you want to try.... First try in the waking state. When you succeed in the waking, then you will be able to succeed in the dreaming because dreaming is deeper, more effort will be needed. And it is also difficult because what to do in a dream and how to do it?

For the dreaming state, Gurdjieff developed a beautiful method. It is one of the old Tibetan methods, and Tibetan seekers have worked very deeply into the dreamworld.

The method is: just falling into sleep you try to remember one thing, any one thing... just a roseflower. Just visualize a roseflower and just go on thinking that you will see it in the dream. Visualize it and go on thinking that in the dream, whatsoever the dream, this roseflower must be there. Visualize its color, its scent, everything. Feel it so it will become alive inside you, and with that roseflower fall into sleep.

Within a few days you will be able to bring that flower into your dream. This is a great success, because now you have created at least a part of the dream. Now you are the master. At least one part of the dream, the flower, has come. And the moment you see the flower you will immediately remember, "This is a dream." Nothing else is need-ed. The flower and, "This is a dream" have become associ-ated because you have created the flower in the dream. And you were continuously thinking for this flower to appear in the dream and the flower has appeared. Immediately you will recognize, "This is a dream," and the whole quality of the dream will change, the flower-dream and everything around the dream. You have become alert.

Then you can enjoy the dream in a new way—just like a film. And then if you want to stop the dream you can simply stop, put it off. But that will take a little more time and more practice. And then you can create your own dreams. There is no need to be a victim of dreams: you can create your own dreams, you can live your own dreams. You can have a theme just before you fall into sleep, you can direct your dreams just like a film director and you can create a theme out of it.

Tibetans have used dream creations because through dream creation you can change your total mind, the structure. And when you succeed in dreams then you can succeed in sleep. But there is no technique for sleep because there is no content. A technique can work only with a content. Because there is no content, no technique can help. But through dream you will learn to be aware and that awareness can be carried on into sleep.

The last sutra:
Memory is the calling up of past experiences.

These are definitions. He is clarifying things so later on you need not get mixed up.

What is memory?—calling up of past experiences. Continuously, memory is happening. Whenever you see something, immediately memory comes in and distorts it. You have seen me before. You see me again—immediately memory comes in. If you had seen me five years before then the picture of five years, the past picture, will come into your eyes and fill your eyes—and you will see me through that picture.

That's why if you have not seen your friend for many days, the moment you see him you immediately say, "You are looking very thin," or "You are looking very unhealthy," or "You have gathered fat." Immediately! Why?—because you are comparing, the memory has come in. The man himself is not aware that he has gathered fat or he has become thin, but you become aware because immediately you can compare. The past, the last picture comes in, and immediately you can compare.

And this memory is continuously there, being projected on everything you see. This past memory has to be dropped. It should not be a constant interference in your knowing because it doesn't allow you to know the new. You always know in the pattern of the old. It doesn't allow you to feel the new, it makes everything old and rotten. Because of this memory, everybody is bored; the whole humanity is bored. Look at anybody's face—he is bored, bored to death. There is nothing new, no ecstasy.

Why are children so ecstatic? And you cannot imagine how this ecstasy is happening for such simple things. Just a few colored stones on the beach and they start dancing. What is happening to them? Why can't you dance?—because you know those are just stones, your memory is there. For those children there is no memory, those stones are a new phenomenon—as if they have reached to the moon.

I was reading, when the first man reached the moon there was excitement all over the world. And everybody was looking at their TV's—but within fifteen minutes everybody was bored, finished: "What to do now? The man is walking on the moon." After just fifteen minutes—and this dream had taken millions of years to reach there—and now nobody was interested in what was happening.

Everything becomes old. Immediately it becomes memory, it

becomes old. If you can drop your memories... dropping doesn't mean that you cease to remember, dropping only means dropping this constant interference. When you need it you can pull it back into focus. When you don't need it just let it be there, silent, not continuously coming.

The past, if continuously present, will not allow the present to be. And if you miss the present you miss all.

Enough for today?